THE NEW WESSEX SELECTION OF THOMAS HARDY'S POETRY

THE NEW WESSEX EDITIONS
The Novels of Thomas Hardy
General Editor P. N. Furbank

The Stories of Thomas Hardy
edited by F. B. Pinion

The Complete Poems of Thomas Hardy
edited by James Gibson

The Dynasts
edited by Harold Orel

THE NEW WESSEX SELECTION OF THOMAS HARDY'S POETRY

*Chosen by John and Eirian Wain
and introduced by John Wain*

PAPERMAC

ISBN 0-333-51626-5

First published 1978 by
MACMILLAN LONDON LIMITED
London and Basingstoke

*Associated companies in Auckland, Delhi,
Dublin, Gaborone, Hamburg, Harare, Hong
Kong, Johannesburg, Kuala Lumpur, Lagos,
Manzini, Melbourne, Mexico City, Nairobi,
New York, Singapore and Tokyo*

*Second impression 1982
Reprinted 1985 (twice)*

*Papermac edition 1989
Reprinted 1990 (twice), 1991*

Printed in Hong Kong

CONTENTS

6

8

INTRODUCTION

THOMAS HARDY's father and grandfather were each named Thomas
Hardy. The first two T.H.s were both in the building trade and both
had musical tastes; Hardy the First led the church choir at Stinsford
('Mellstock' in his grandson's Wessex); Hardy the Second played the
violin at village feasts and dances. In childhood, Hardy the Third would
dance rapturously to the tune of his father's fiddle. All this showed up
when in due course he became one of the greatest poets of the English
language. His approach to poetry was partly that of a craftsman
(he himself was trained as a draughtsman and an architect) and partly
of a singer and dancer to music. His work has a double importance.
It is the record of an individual mind of great strength and deep
originality; and it is also the channel whereby a vital popular tradition
flows from a remote rural past to our modern urban world.

I

Mediaeval lyric is still very close to folk-song; plainly visible are its
roots in that group activity which comes naturally to agricultural
peoples at seasons of harvest when unaccustomed leisure and abundant
food produce a mood of exultation, or when their long days of toil
unite them in certain physical movements, reaping, flailing, sowing,
pulling on oars or ropes. The basis of all such lyric is the solo voice of
the song-leader interspersed with the refrain of the chorus; and, since
all lyric poetry is related to dance as well as to song, the intricate
recurring rhythms and rhymes of lyric verse also have their organic
roots in group activity, in the rhythms of work and festival. These
qualities cling to them even when social change has abolished the
conditions under which the original pattern was laid down. There is a
modern parallel in the blues, developed by a black working class whose
labour was predominantly agricultural; many of its features survive
in the urban mutations of rock and pop, eagerly consumed by a
generation of youngsters who have hardly so much as seen a ploughed
field.

The richness of mediaeval lyric poetry is maintained without
faltering during the Tudor generations, when the life of the populace
barely altered from its mediaeval pattern. After that, increasingly, it
became sporadic, surviving better in traditional agricultural areas,

dying out by the end of the eighteenth century under the new conditions of industrialism. By the middle years of the nineteenth century, if we are looking for a survival of that mediaeval lyric grace as it comes down through Elizabethan, Jacobean and Caroline England, we shall find it most easily in the 'backward' areas, however far distant; the kind of English people who crossed the Atlantic, many of them against their will as transported felons or starving surplus labour, and subsequently provided the poor white population of the Appalachian mountains and the valleys of West Virginia, kept alive late mediaeval ballads and Elizabethan lyrics long enough to perform them to the astonished ears of twentieth-century collectors.

Hardy's unique place in English poetry has its basis here. His area of England, the south-west, was agricultural and conservative; he grew up in a tradition of village singing and dancing, of village musicians in church, 'bowing it higher and higher', of jigs, reels, airs and come-all-ye's. It is this that sets him so much apart from the main current of English poetry in his time. There are very few other poets of the later nineteenth century, still less of the early twentieth, whom he in any way resembles. Now and again he shows the influence of Browning (usually disastrous) or Swinburne (hardly less so), and there is a deep natural affinity with the Dorset poet William Barnes. But the real roots of Hardy's poetry are the tough, clinging, gnarled but still green and flowing roots of English popular lyric verse. If we want something that resembles a typical Hardy poem we shall find it more easily between the fourteenth and the sixteenth centuries than in his own bowler-hatted epoch. The poets who wrote

> *O mistress, why*
> *Outcast am I*
> *All utterly*
> *From your pleasance;*
> *Sith ye and I*
> *Or this truly*   Or: ere
> *Familiarly*   (ere this = formerly)
> *Have had pastance*
> *And lovingly*
> *Ye would apply*
> *My company*
> *To my comfort?*
> *But now truly*
> *Unlovingly*

> *Ye do deny*
> *Me to resort.*

or,

> *Rutterkin is come unto our town*
> *In a cloak without coat or gown,*
> *Save ragged hood to cover his crown,*
>   *Like a rutterkin, hoyda, hoyda!*
>
> *Rutterkin can speak no English;*
> *His tongue runneth all on buttered fish,*
> *Besmeared with grease about his dish,*
>   *Like a rutterkin, hoyda, hoyda!*
>
> *Rutterkin shall bring you all good luck,*
> *A stoup of beer up at a pluck,*
> *Till his brain be wise as a duck,*
>   *Like a rutterkin, hoyda, hoyda!*

or,

> *Weep you no more, sad fountains;*
>   *What need you flow so fast?*
> *Look how the snowy mountains*
>   *Heaven's sun doth gently waste!*
> *But my Sun's heavenly eyes*
>   *View not your weeping,*
>   *That now lies sleeping*
> *Softly, now softly lies*
>   *Sleeping.*
>
> *Sleep is a reconciling,*
>   *A rest that peace begets;*
> *Doth not the sun rise smiling*
>   *When fair at even he sets?*
> *Rest you then, rest, sad eyes!*
>   *Melt not in weeping,*
>   *While she lies sleeping*
> *Softly, now softly lies*
>   *Sleeping.*

– these unknown poets were Hardy's masters, less because he consciously imitated them than because they established the tradition in which it was natural for him to work. By a supremely fortunate chance, a poet with immense technical skill and a beautifully sensitive ear was plugged in to a popular, unsophisticated tradition which had always maintained a commerce with high, 'literary' poetry for the printed page, but never at the cost of its own identity.

Hardy was unquestionably a lyric poet; lyrical and reflective. His dramatic blank verse does not represent his genius nearly so well, and *The Dynasts* comes to life chiefly at those points where the action is clinched or commented on in lyric vein. Now, appreciating and enjoying lyric poetry is largely a matter of being alive to its blend of elements. Starting from the relatively simple group-activity of song and chorus, movement and dance, it moves always towards the personal and unique. When lyric forms are adapted, as they always are, to the expression of those thoughts a man has when he is meditating in solitude, we are in the presence of a hybrid that owes a great deal to both parents. Now and again these unknown mediaeval poets throw off a lyric which is immortal, blending a personal emotion with a shared form, that has the fragile delicacy of a soap-bubble. These are the lyrics we all know, 'Sumer is icumen in,' or 'Foweles in the frith', or 'The maidens came/When I was in my mother's bower' with its refrain 'The bailey beareth the bell away'. When we read and marvel at these things we are very close to Hardy's poetry, which combines the deeply personal with the deeply shared, and which wears its raiment of long tradition as unselfconsciously as an old jacket.

II

It is, in fact, an important part of Hardy's temperament that he feels at home with tradition, likes the presence of things that have weathered and endured. His imagination responds to customs and beliefs and societies that have lived on through the generations, and also to the immensities of geological time; he muses on the contrast between the frail thing of blood and bones and nerves that is a human being, and the unimaginable age of the earth he walks on. Not necessarily to draw the conclusion that human life is insignificant by the side of these ancient works of creation – sometimes, indeed, virtually the opposite:

> *Primaeval rocks form the road's steep border,*
> *And much have they faced there, first and last,*
> *Of the transitory in Earth's long order;*
> *But what they record in colour and cast*
> *Is – that we two passed.*

Many, though by no means all, of Hardy's poems were written in later life – he is one of the many exceptions to the once-prevalent Romantic view that poets are at their best in flaming youth and subsequently decline steeply – and he characteristically approaches his subjects down a perspective of memory. For all of us except those who die very young, all experience is a twice-told tale: there is the event as it actually happened and as it affected us at the time, and the event as we recall it in the light of later knowledge and later development within ourselves. When we muse on our experience and re-create it in memory, we become very like ghosts haunting the scenes of former action. It is this strand in Hardy that makes him so sympathetic to the idea of ghosts and hauntings. He is on record as saying (in the *Life* published under his second wife's name but evidently written mostly by himself):

'. . . if there is any way of getting a melancholy satisfaction out of life, it lies in dying, so to speak, before one is out of the flesh; by which I mean putting on the manners of ghosts, wandering in their haunts, and taking their views of surrounding things. To think of life as passing away is a sadness: to think of it as past is at least tolerable.'

He likes, and this may be an overlap between Hardy the poet and Hardy the novelist, to reflect on the way things have turned out, the endless *sequelae* of life, what T. S. Eliot calls 'The trailing consequences of further days and ways'. Very much a poet of the emotions, he describes with particular accuracy the strange, patchy and unpredictable way in which they persist; the youthful emotions, in an ageing person, do not die down steadily in a long tranquil curve, but gutter out and flare up like a dying fire on a gusty night: so

> . . . time, to make me grieve,
> Part steals, lets part abide;
> And shakes this fragile frame at eve
> With throbbings of noontide.

Or consider the old dame in his narrative poem 'The Dance at the Phœnix', who re-lives her flirtatious girlhood for one deliciously mad evening and then gets back into bed and dies before morning – a memorable haunting!

These two features of Hardy's mind – his sympathy with the old and the traditional, and the fact that he is a poet of the emotions rather than of ideas – go far to account for his gentle tolerance, in the poems, of beliefs and customs that run counter to his actual convictions. As a young man he lost the religious faith of his childhood, and there is plenty of evidence throughout his work, in fiction and poetry, that he was a cosmic pessimist, had no belief in a personal and beneficent God or in the survival of identity after death; further, that he considered the social structure that had assembled itself round a core of Christian belief as rigid and often cruel, like plaster of Paris round a living limb. Yet when, in his poems, he contemplates simple people with an unquestioned faith, he never feels superior to them or encourages the reader to feel so. Their church-going and music-making are seen as a natural part of their lives, and so are their beliefs. In 'The Lost Pyx', for instance, he recounts a mediaeval Christian legend, with a full sense of its magic and its tenderness.

This magic and tenderness are not narrowly caught within the bounds of human religion; they include nature, they bring the animal creation inside the welcoming circle of belief in a way that formal Christianity has not always managed to do. When the distractedly searching priest finally comes on the pyx which contains the sacrament symbolising the body of Christ, he finds it surrounded by animals, wild as well as domestic, gazing at it 'in pause profound'. Obviously the legend is attractive to Hardy, just as the folk-belief that the cattle go down on their knees in the byre on Christmas Eve at midnight is attractive. He has an instinctive reverence for all life, a humility before its continuous miracle, and his countryman's familiarity with birds and animals is irradiated by pity for their frequent sufferings. In 'Afterwards', probably his most celebrated poem, he surveys the natural universe that he will leave when he dies, and as well as its sublimities and immensities he finds room for the hedgehog travelling furtively over the lawn on a summer night – not forgetting to add the thought that, while the stars and the seasons will get along perfectly well without him, the hedgehog needs protection which he wishes he could give more effectively.

III

Time, traditions, customs, beliefs, rocks, landscapes, birds and animals – but always with, in Dryden's phrase, 'the diapason closing full in Man'. The core of Hardy's poetry, like that of any other poet, is his treatment of the human being. And this is compassionate, wry, rueful, ironic, satirical, even hilarious, as the behaviour of these wayward creatures provokes each reaction in turn. Needless to say, he writes a great deal about the relations of the sexes; most writers, like most non-writers, find sexual love the most interesting and memorable part of life, but Hardy even more than most; a stout volume could be made of his poems on this theme alone. He ranges over the whole gamut of feeling, from the yearning note of 'To Lizbie Browne' to the mordant laughter of 'The Ruined Maid'; from a song of the happiness of love ('When I Set Out for Lyonnesse') to a tender and sympathetic description of how that love can come flooding back unexpectedly in later years ('A Church Romance'). In a central position among his poems about love, the Everest of this whole range, is of course the high and passionate sequence (pages 103-123) he wrote after his first wife's death in 1912. Their relationship had been a difficult one; for various reasons his love for her had never been able to flow freely while she lived; not long after her death he revisited the little Cornish town of St Juliot where he had met and wooed her, and the cliffs and coves where they had wandered – and suddenly, sweeping all before them like great explosions of lava, the poems came pouring out.

These poems of 1912-13, taken as a whole, make one of the glories of English literature. As expressions of love, regret, tenderness, need, they are fit to stand beside Shakespeare's Sonnets. It is true that the Sonnets have extra dimensions, expressing revulsion, jealousy and sexual craving, all of which would have been out of place in Hardy's elegiac sequence; but there is not much difference in intensity, in fire, in artistry. Every critic has recognised that this sequence is Hardy's greatest achievement in poetry (and is it really matched anywhere in the novels?), but not every critic has been equally successful in putting into words the reasons why they move the reader so powerfully. The most successful (that I have come across, at any rate) is W. W. Robson in his brief but brilliant *Modern English Literature* (Oxford, 1970):

This series of poems . . . is elegiac and tragic; at the same time, it is full of the ardour and passion of love. Hardy's thoughts are fixed on the dead, but he is not necrophiliac or morbid. What mattered was that he had lived, and she had lived, and they had once loved. Reliving their life together, he is filled with grief, but also with joy. As he realises the co-presence of these emotions, he is struck with terror and anguish. That *vanishing* of someone we love, so sadly familiar an experience, yet so inexplicable and terrible, Hardy conveys as no other poet has done, in the greatest of his poems, 'The Going'.

A critic of Mr Robson's authority is entitled to his confident judgements, and 'The Going' may well be Hardy's greatest single poem; though I find, personally, that there are ten or a dozen that occupy the very topmost pinnacle, and 'the best' is always the one I have just finished reading. Hardy's vast output is, naturally, uneven, and yet it is surprising how rarely one comes across a Hardy poem that could fairly be called bad. Even poems marred by clumsiness, or snarled up in those elaborate grammatical and syntactical constructions that sometimes make them as hard to sort out as a poem in Latin, are never commonplace or boring. The poet's mind is always at work, always on its own deeply original level. Very much a poet of ordinary life, he sees what the rest of us see, but never without some fresh, unexpected angle, some play of light that makes the familiar new and intriguing. Even in poems which we have, without much regret, screened out of this selection, there are those Hardean quirks of insight, those fancies which at first seem merely odd but very soon enter one's mind and establish their essential truthfulness.

A writer's working materials are his perception of life and his command of language. Hardy approaches life and language in the same way – like a carpenter handling wood, working with it and not against it, never disguising the grain or even the knot-holes, letting the material itself help to shape the final product. He loved the stubborn, anarchic selfhood of things, the unpredictable happenings, the odd ways in which life turned out, the kinks and corrugations that nothing could iron out of the human being. And his language is the same – sometimes plain and direct, sometimes odd and stilted, here a Dorset dialect word, there a Latinism, elsewhere a coinage of his own. The grain and the knot-holes are there for all to see, just as they are in daily experience.

Modern poetry is mostly urban. It comes from the polyglot confusion, the mechanical haste, the anonymity and loneliness, of the big cities. In a world so dominated by these things, and so committed to expressing them in its art, the continued popularity of Hardy's poetry often seems strange. His work runs completely counter to all the orthodoxies of modern literature and art; it is local, leisurely, handcrafted; it deals with village gossip and the emotions that make or mar ordinary lives. *The Dynasts*, it is true, uses a huge canvas to embody a vision of history; but, though it has many admirers, it is not *The Dynasts* that keeps Hardy among the most loved of English poets; it is the lyrics, the tender, brooding poems of memory, the satires of circumstance. And perhaps, after all, it is not strange that these poems should command such a wide public as year follows year. The mere fact that they are not machine-made, not gadgets thrown off by the restless energy of Megalopolis, gives them a vitality that we respond to. Though Hardy's tone varies so widely, it is always the voice of a countryman we are hearing. Country people, in those days and even to some extent now, live and work in direct contact with natural materials, with animals, with the weather, and this gives their speech a directness and concreteness unlikely to be developed by pushing knobs on a computer. Along with this, the countryman has a tendency to measured, slightly formal speech. When he wants to say something particularly important, he instinctively chooses words and constructions that, by comparison with the hurried slanginess of urban language, seem slightly old-fashioned, slightly formal. A poet of our own day, Peter Levi, has remarked that Hardy's poems, with their blend of rural simplicity and a traditional, somewhat quaint formality, are like the painted wooden horses at a fairground. This seems to me admirable, one poet finding the perfect image for another's work; especially as Levi, who loves and admires Hardy's poetry, would be the last to deny that at any moment one of these homely, stylized, varnished creatures is capable of spreading the wings of Pegasus and carrying us off through the skies.

March 1977   JOHN WAIN

PUBLISHER'S NOTE

The text of Hardy's poems in this selection is that of the New Wessex *Complete Poems of Thomas Hardy* edited by James Gibson (Macmillan 1976). For convenience' sake, the system of numbering established by Mr Gibson has been retained, and the poems appear in the same order, though not consecutively, as they do in *The Complete Poems*.

1 Domicilium

IT faces west, and round the back and sides
High beeches, bending, hang a veil of boughs,
And sweep against the roof. Wild honeysucks
Climb on the walls, and seem to sprout a wish
(If we may fancy wish of trees and plants)
To overtop the apple-trees hard by.

Red roses, lilacs, variegated box
Are there in plenty, and such hardy flowers
As flourish best untrained. Adjoining these
Are herbs and esculents; and farther still
A field; then cottages with trees, and last
The distant hills and sky.

Behind, the scene is wilder. Heath and furze
Are everything that seems to grow and thrive
Upon the uneven ground. A stunted thorn
Stands here and there, indeed; and from a pit
An oak uprises, springing from a seed
Dropped by some bird a hundred years ago.

                      In days bygone –
Long gone – my father's mother, who is now
Blest with the blest, would take me out to walk.
At such a time I once inquired of her
How looked the spot when first she settled here.
The answer I remember. 'Fifty years
Have passed since then, my child, and change has marked
The face of all things. Yonder garden-plots
And orchards were uncultivated slopes
O'ergrown with bramble bushes, furze and thorn:
That road a narrow path shut in by ferns,
Which, almost trees, obscured the passer-by.

'Our house stood quite alone, and those tall firs
And beeches were not planted. Snakes and efts
Swarmed in the summer days, and nightly bats
Would fly about our bedrooms. Heathcroppers
Lived on the hills, and were our only friends;
So wild it was when first we settled here.'

9 Neutral Tones

WE stood by a pond that winter day,
And the sun was white, as though chidden of God,
And a few leaves lay on the starving sod;
    – They had fallen from an ash, and were gray.

Your eyes on me were as eyes that rove
Over tedious riddles of years ago;
And some words played between us to and fro
    On which lost the more by our love.

The smile on your mouth was the deadest thing
Alive enough to have strength to die;
And a grin of bitterness swept thereby
    Like an ominous bird a-wing. . . .

Since then, keen lessons that love deceives,
And wrings with wrong, have shaped to me
Your face, and the God-curst sun, and a tree,
    And a pond edged with grayish leaves.

1867

10 She at His Funeral

THEY bear him to his resting-place –
In slow procession sweeping by;
I follow at a stranger's space;
His kindred they, his sweetheart I.

Unchanged my gown of garish dye,
Though sable-sad is their attire;
But they stand round with griefless eye,
Whilst my regret consumes like fire!

187–

12 Her Dilemma

(In —— Church)

THE two were silent in a sunless church,
Whose mildewed walls, uneven paving-stones,
And wasted carvings passed antique research;
And nothing broke the clock's dull monotones.

Leaning against a wormy poppy-head,
So wan and worn that he could scarcely stand,
– For he was soon to die, – he softly said,
'Tell me you love me!' – holding long her hand.

She would have given a world to breathe 'yes' truly,
So much his life seemed hanging on her mind,
And hence she lied, her heart persuaded throughly
'Twas worth her soul to be a moment kind.

But the sad need thereof, his nearing death,
So mocked humanity that she shamed to prize
A world conditioned thus, or care for breath
Where Nature such dilemmas could devise.

1866

14 She, to Him I

WHEN you shall see me in the toils of Time,
My lauded beauties carried off from me,
My eyes no longer stars as in their prime,
My name forgot of Maiden Fair and Free;

When, in your being, heart concedes to mind,
And judgment, though you scarce its process know,
Recalls the excellencies I once enshrined,
And you are irked that they have withered so:

Remembering mine the loss is, not the blame,
That Sportsman Time but rears his brood to kill,
Knowing me in my soul the very same –
One who would die to spare you touch of ill! –
Will you not grant to old affection's claim
The hand of friendship down Life's sunless hill?

1866

15 She, to Him II

PERHAPS, long hence, when I have passed away,
Some other's feature, accent, thought like mine,
Will carry you back to what I used to say,
And bring some memory of your love's decline.

Then you may pause awhile and think, 'Poor jade!'
And yield a sigh to me – as ample due,
Not as the tittle of a debt unpaid
To one who could resign her all to you –

And thus reflecting, you will never see
That your thin thought, in two small words conveyed,
Was no such fleeting phantom-thought to me,
But the Whole Life wherein my part was played;
And you amid its fitful masquerade
A Thought – as I in your life seem to be!

1866

16 *She, to Him* III

I WILL be faithful to thee; aye, I will!
And Death shall choose me with a wondering eye
That he did not discern and domicile
One his by right ever since that last Good-bye!

I have no care for friends, or kin, or prime
Of manhood who deal gently with me here;
Amid the happy people of my time
Who work their love's fulfilment, I appear

Numb as a vane that cankers on its point,
True to the wind that kissed ere canker came:
Despised by souls of Now, who would disjoint
The mind from memory, making Life all aim,

My old dexterities in witchery gone,
And nothing left for Love to look upon.

1866

17 *She, to Him* IV

THIS love puts all humanity from me;
I can but maledict her, pray her dead,
For giving love and getting love of thee –
Feeding a heart that else mine own had fed!

How much I love I know not, life not known,
Save as one unit I would add love by;
But this I know, my being is but thine own –
Fused from its separateness by ecstasy.

And thus I grasp thy amplitudes, of her
Ungrasped, though helped by nigh-regarding eyes;
Canst thou then hate me as an envier
Who see unrecked what I so dearly prize?
Believe me, Lost One, Love is lovelier
The more it shapes its moan in selfish-wise.

1866

18 Ditty

(E.L.G.)

BENEATH a knap where flown
        Nestlings play,
Within walls of weathered stone,
        Far away
From the files of formal houses,
By the bough the firstling browses,
Lives a Sweet: no merchants meet,
No man barters, no man sells
        Where she dwells.

Upon that fabric fair
        'Here is she!'
Seems written everywhere
        Unto me.
But to friends and nodding neighbours,
Fellow-wights in lot and labours,
Who descry the times as I,
No such lucid legend tells
        Where she dwells.

Should I lapse to what I was
        Ere we met;
(Such will not be, but because
        Some forget
Let me feign it) – none would notice
That where she I know by rote is
Spread a strange and withering change,
Like a drying of the wells
        Where she dwells.

To feel I might have kissed –
        Loved as true –
Otherwhere, nor Mine have missed
        My life through,
Had I never wandered near her,
Is a smart severe – severer
In the thought that she is nought,

Even as I, beyond the dells
        Where she dwells.

And Devotion droops her glance
        To recall
What bond-servants of Chance
        We are all.
I but found her in that, going
On my errant path unknowing,
I did not out-skirt the spot
That no spot on earth excels,
        – Where she dwells!

1870

21 *San Sebastian*

(*August 1813*)

WITH THOUGHTS OF SERGEANT M—— (PENSIONER), WHO DIED 185-

'WHY, Sergeant, stray on the Ivel Way,
As though at home there were spectres rife?
From first to last 'twas a proud career!
And your sunny years with a gracious wife
        Have brought you a daughter dear.

'I watched her to-day; a more comely maid,
As she danced in her muslin bowed with blue,
Round a Hintock maypole never gayed.'
– 'Aye, aye; I watched her this day, too,
        As it happens,' the Sergeant said.

'My daughter is now,' he again began,
'Of just such an age as one I knew
When we of the Line, the Forlorn-hope van,
On an August morning – a chosen few –
        Stormed San Sebastian.

'She's a score less three; so about was *she* –
The maiden I wronged in Peninsular days. . . .
You may prate of your prowess in lusty times,
But as years gnaw inward you blink your bays,
    And see too well your crimes!

'We'd stormed it at night, by the flapping light
Of burning towers, and the mortar's boom:
We'd topped the breach; but had failed to stay,
For our files were misled by the baffling gloom;
    And we said we'd storm by day.

'So, out of the trenches, with features set,
On that hot, still morning, in measured pace,
Our column climbed; climbed higher yet,
Passed the fauss'bray, scarp, up the curtain-face,
    And along the parapet.

'From the batteried hornwork the cannoneers
Hove crashing balls of iron fire;
On the shaking gap mount the volunteers
In files, and as they mount expire
    Amid curses, groans, and cheers.

'Five hours did we storm, five hours re-form,
As Death cooled those hot blood pricked on;
Till our cause was helped by a woe within:
They were blown from the summit we'd leapt upon,
    And madly we entered in.

'On end for plunder, 'mid rain and thunder
That burst with the lull of our cannonade,
We vamped the streets in the stifling air –
Our hunger unsoothed, our thirst unstayed –
    And ransacked the buildings there.

'From the shady vaults of their walls of white
We rolled rich puncheons of Spanish grape,
Till at length, with the fire of the wine alight,
I saw at a doorway a fair fresh shape –
    A woman, a sylph, or sprite.

'Afeard she fled, and with heated head
I pursued to the chamber she called her own;
– When might is right no qualms deter,
And having her helpless and alone
     I wreaked my will on her.

'She raised her beseeching eyes to me,
And I heard the words of prayer she sent
In her own soft language. . . . Fatefully
I copied those eyes for my punishment
     In begetting the girl you see!

'So, to-day I stand with a God-set brand
Like Cain's, when he wandered from kindred's ken. . . .
I served through the war that made Europe free;
I wived me in peace-year. But, hid from men,
     I bear that mark on me.

'Maybe we shape our offspring's guise
From fancy, or we know not what,
And that no deep impression dies, –
For the mother of my child is not
     The mother of her eyes.

'And I nightly stray on the Ivel Way
As though at home there were spectres rife;
I delight me not in my proud career;
And 'tis coals of fire that a gracious wife
     Should have brought me a daughter dear!'

26 The Alarm

(Traditional)

IN MEMORY OF ONE OF THE WRITER'S FAMILY WHO WAS A VOLUNTEER
DURING THE WAR WITH NAPOLEON

IN a ferny byway
   Near the great South-Wessex Highway,
A homestead raised its breakfast-smoke aloft;
The dew-damps still lay steamless, for the sun had made no skyway,
      And twilight cloaked the croft.

   It was almost past conceiving
   Here, where woodbines hung inweaving,
That quite closely hostile armaments might steer,
Save from seeing in the porchway a fair woman mutely grieving,
      And a harnessed Volunteer.

   In haste he'd flown there
   To his comely wife alone there,
While marching south hard by, to still her fears,
For she soon would be a mother, and few messengers were known
      there
      In these campaigning years.

   'Twas time to be Good-bying,
   Since the assembly-hour was nighing
In royal George's town at six that morn;
And betwixt its wharves and this retreat were ten good miles of
      hieing
      Ere ring of bugle-horn.

   'I've laid in food, Dear,
   And broached the spiced and brewed, Dear;
And if our July hope should antedate,
Let the char-wench mount and gallop by the halterpath and wood,
      Dear,
      And fetch assistance straight.

   'As for Buonaparte, forget him;
   He's not like to land! But let him,

Those strike with aim who strike for wives and sons!
And the war-boats built to float him; 'twere but wanted to upset
          him
          A slat from Nelson's guns!

          'But, to assure thee,
          And of creeping fears to cure thee,
     If he *should* be rumoured anchoring in the Road,
Drive with the nurse to Kingsbere; and let nothing thence allure
          thee
          Till we have him safe-bestowed.

          'Now, to turn to marching matters: –
          I've my knapsack, firelock, spatters,
     Crossbelts, priming-horn, stock, bay'net, blackball, clay,
Pouch, magazine, and flint-box that at every quick-step clatters; –
          My heart, Dear; that must stay!'

          – With breathings broken
          Farewell was kissed unspoken,
     And they parted there as morning stroked the panes;
And the Volunteer went on, and turned, and twirled his glove for
          token,
          And took the coastward lanes.

          When above He'th Hills he found him,
          He saw, on gazing round him,
     The Barrow-Beacon burning – burning low,
As if, perhaps, enkindled ever since he'd homeward bound him;
          And it meant: Expect the Foe!

          Leaving the byway,
          He entered on the highway,
     Where were cars and chariots, faring fast inland;
'He's anchored, Soldier!' shouted some: 'God save thee,
          marching thy way,
          Th'lt front him on the strand!'

          He slowed; he stopped; he paltered
          Awhile with self, and faltered,

'Why courting misadventure shoreward roam?
To Molly, surely! Seek the woods with her till times have altered;
    Charity favours home.

    'Else, my denying
    He'd come, she'll read as lying –
Think the Barrow-Beacon must have met my eyes –
That my words were not unwareness, but deceit of her, while
    vying
    In deeds that jeopardize.

    'At home is stocked provision,
    And to-night, without suspicion,
We might bear it with us to a covert near;
Such sin, to save a childing wife, would earn it Christ's remission,
    Though none forgive it here!'

    While he stood thinking,
    A little bird, perched drinking
Among the crowfoot tufts the river bore,
Was tangled in their stringy arms and fluttered, almost sinking
    Near him, upon the moor.

    He stepped in, reached, and seized it,
    And, preening, had released it
But that a thought of Holy Writ occurred,
And Signs Divine ere battle, till it seemed him Heaven had pleased it
    As guide to send the bird.

    'O Lord, direct me! . . .
    Doth Duty now expect me
To march a-coast, or guard my weak ones near?
Give this bird a flight according, that I thence learn to elect me
    The southward or the rear.'

    He loosed his clasp; when, rising,
    The bird – as if surmising –
Bore due to southward, crossing by the Froom,
And Durnover Great Field and Fort, the soldier clear advising –
    Prompted he deemed by Whom.

Then on he panted
By grim Mai-Don, and slanted
Up the steep Ridge-way, hearkening between whiles;
Till nearing coast and harbour he beheld the shore-line planted
With Foot and Horse for miles.

Mistrusting not the omen,
He gained the beach, where Yeomen,
Militia, Fencibles and Pikemen bold,
With Regulars in thousands, were enmassed to meet the Foemen,
Whose fleet had not yet shoaled.

Captain and Colonel,
Sere Generals, Ensigns vernal,
Were there; of neighbour-natives, Michel, Smith,
Meggs, Bingham, Gambier, Cunningham, to face the said nocturnal
Swoop on their land and kith.

But Buonaparte still tarried:
His project had miscarried;
At the last hour, equipped for victory,
The fleet had paused; his subtle combinations had been parried
By British strategy.

Homeward returning
Anon, no beacons burning,
No alarms, the Volunteer, in modest bliss,
Te Deum sang with wife and friends: 'We praise Thee, Lord, discerning
That Thou hast helped in this!'

To Jenny came a gentle youth
    From inland leazes lone,
His love was fresh as apple-blooth
    By Parrett, Yeo, or Tone.
And duly he entreated her
To be his tender minister,
    And take him for her own.

Now Jenny's life had hardly been
    A life of modesty;
And few in Casterbridge had seen
    More loves of sorts than she
From scarcely sixteen years above;
Among them sundry troopers of
    The King's-Own Cavalry.

But each with charger, sword, and gun,
    Had bluffed the Biscay wave;
And Jenny prized her rural one
    For all the love he gave.
She vowed to be, if they were wed,
His honest wife in heart and head
    From bride-ale hour to grave.

Wedded they were. Her husband's trust
    In Jenny knew no bound,
And Jenny kept her pure and just,
    Till even malice found
No sin or sign of ill to be
In one who walked so decently
    The duteous helpmate's round.

Two sons were born, and bloomed to men,
    And roamed, and were as not:
Alone was Jenny left again
    As ere her mind had sought
A solace in domestic joys,
And ere the vanished pair of boys
    Were sent to sun her cot.

She numbered near on sixty years,
    And passed as elderly,
When, on a day, with flushing fears,
    She learnt from shouts of glee,
And shine of swords, and thump of drum,
Her early loves from war had come,
    The King's-Own Cavalry.

She turned aside, and bowed her head
    Anigh Saint Peter's door;
'Alas for chastened thoughts!' she said;
    'I'm faded now, and hoar,
And yet those notes – they thrill me through,
And those gay forms move me anew
    As they moved me of yore!' . . .

'Twas Christmas, and the Phœnix Inn
    Was lit with tapers tall,
For thirty of the trooper men
    Had vowed to give a ball
As 'Theirs' had done ('twas handed down)
When lying in the selfsame town
    Ere Buonaparté's fall.

That night the throbbing 'Soldier's Joy',
    The measured tread and sway
Of 'Fancy-Lad' and 'Maiden Coy',
    Reached Jenny as she lay
Beside her spouse; till springtide blood
Seemed scouring through her like a flood
    That whisked the years away.

She rose, arrayed, and decked her head
    Where the bleached hairs grew thin;
Upon her cap two bows of red
    She fixed with hasty pin;
Unheard descending to the street
She trod the flags with tune-led feet,
    And stood before the Inn.

Save for the dancers', not a sound
    Disturbed the icy air;

No watchman on his midnight round
    Or traveller was there;
But over All-Saints', high and bright,
Pulsed to the music Sirius white,
    The Wain by Bullstake Square.

She knocked, but found her further stride
    Checked by a sergeant tall:
'Gay Granny, whence come you?' he cried;
    'This is a private ball.'
– 'No one has more right here than me!
Ere you were born, man,' answered she,
    'I knew the regiment all!'

'Take not the lady's visit ill!'
    The steward said; 'for see,
We lack sufficient partners still,
    So, prithee, let her be!'
They seized and whirled her mid the maze,
And Jenny felt as in the days
    Of her immodesty.

Hour chased each hour, and night advanced;
    She sped as shod with wings;
Each time and every time she danced –
    Reels, jigs, poussettes, and flings:
They cheered her as she soared and swooped,
(She had learnt ere art in dancing drooped
    From hops to slothful swings).

The favourite Quick-step 'Speed the Plough' –
    (Cross hands, cast off, and wheel) –
'The Triumph', 'Sylph', 'The Row-dow-dow',
    Famed 'Major Malley's Reel',
'The Duke of York's', 'The Fairy Dance',
'The Bridge of Lodi' (brought from France),
    She beat out, toe and heel.

The 'Fall of Paris' clanged its close,
    And Peter's chime went four,

When Jenny, bosom-beating, rose
    To seek her silent door.
They tiptoed in escorting her,
Lest stroke of heel or clink of spur
    Should break her goodman's snore.

The fire that lately burnt fell slack
    When lone at last was she;
Her nine-and-fifty years came back;
    She sank upon her knee
Beside the durn, and like a dart
A something arrowed through her heart
    In shoots of agony.

Their footsteps died as she leant there,
    Lit by the morning star
Hanging above the moorland, where
    The aged elm-rows are;
As overnight, from Pummery Ridge
To Maembury Ring and Standfast Bridge
    No life stirred, near or far.

Though inner mischief worked amain,
    She reached her husband's side;
Where, toil-weary, as he had lain
    Beneath the patchwork pied
When forthward yestereve she crept,
And as unwitting, still he slept
    Who did in her confide.

A tear sprang as she turned and viewed
    His features free from guile;
She kissed him long, as when, just wooed,
    She chose his domicile
She felt she would give more than life
To be the single-hearted wife
    That she had been erstwhile. . . .

Time wore to six. Her husband rose
    And struck the steel and stone;

He glanced at Jenny, whose repose
    Seemed deeper than his own.
With dumb dismay, on closer sight,
He gathered sense that in the night,
    Or morn, her soul had flown.

When told that some too mighty strain
    For one so many-yeared
Had burst her bosom's master-vein,
    His doubts remained unstirred.
His Jenny had not left his side
Betwixt the eve and morning-tide:
    - The King's said not a word.

Well! times are not as times were then,
    Nor fair ones half so free;
And truly they were martial men,
    The King's-Own Cavalry.
And when they went from Casterbridge
And vanished over Mellstock Ridge,
    'Twas saddest morn to see.

I MARK the months in liveries dank and dry,
  The noontides many-shaped and hued;
    I see the nightfall shades subtrude,
And hear the monotonous hours clang negligently by.

I view the evening bonfires of the sun
  On hills where morning rains have hissed;
    The eyeless countenance of the mist
Pallidly rising when the summer droughts are done.

I have seen the lightning-blade, the leaping star,
  The cauldrons of the sea in storm,
    Have felt the earthquake's lifting arm,
And trodden where abysmal fires and snow-cones are.

I learn to prophesy the hid eclipse,
  The coming of eccentric orbs;
    To mete the dust the sky absorbs,
To weigh the sun, and fix the hour each planet dips.

I witness fellow earth-men surge and strive;
  Assemblies meet, and throb, and part;
    Death's sudden finger, sorrow's smart;
– All the vast various moils that mean a world alive.

But that I fain would wot of shuns my sense –
  Those sights of which old prophets tell,
    Those signs the general word so well
As vouchsafed their unheed, denied my long suspense.

In graveyard green, where his pale dust lies pent
  To glimpse a phantom parent, friend,
    Wearing his smile, and 'Not the end!'
Outbreathing softly: that were blest enlightenment;

Or, if a dead Love's lips, whom dreams reveal
  When midnight imps of King Decay
    Delve sly to solve me back to clay,
Should leave some print to prove her spirit-kisses real;

Or, when Earth's Frail lie bleeding of her Strong,
   If some Recorder, as in Writ,
   Near to the weary scene should flit
And drop one plume as pledge that Heaven inscrolls the wrong.

– There are who, rapt to heights of trancelike trust,
   These tokens claim to feel and see,
   Read radiant hints of times to be –
Of heart to heart returning after dust to dust.

Such scope is granted not to lives like mine . . .
   I have lain in dead men's beds, have walked
   The tombs of those with whom I had talked,
Called many a gone and goodly one to shape a sign,

And panted for response. But none replies;
   No warnings loom, nor whisperings
   To open out my limitings,
And Nescience mutely muses: When a man falls he lies.

36 Friends Beyond

WILLIAM DEWY, Tranter Reuben, Farmer Ledlow late at plough,
   Robert's kin, and John's, and Ned's,
And the Squire, and Lady Susan, lie in Mellstock churchyard now!

'Gone,' I call them, gone for good, that group of local hearts and heads;
   Yet at mothy curfew-tide,
And at midnight when the noon-heat breathes it back from walls and
   leads,

They've a way of whispering to me – fellow-wight who yet abide –
   In the muted, measured note
Of a ripple under archways, or a lone cave's stillicide:

'We have triumphed: this achievement turns the bane to antidote,
   Unsuccesses to success,
Many thought-worn eves and morrows to a morrow free of thought.

'No more need we corn and clothing, feel of old terrestrial stress;
   Chill detraction stirs no sigh;
Fear of death has even bygone us: death gave all that we possess.'

W.D. – 'Ye mid burn the old bass-viol that I set such value by.'
Squire. – 'You may hold the manse in fee,
    You may wed my spouse, may let my children's memory of me
      die.'

Lady S. – 'You may have my rich brocades, my laces; take each
    household key;
    Ransack coffer, desk, bureau;
    Quiz the few poor treasures hid there, con the letters kept by me.'

Far. – 'Ye mid zell my favourite heifer, ye mid let the charlock grow,
    Foul the grinterns, give up thrift.'

Far. Wife. – 'If ye break my best blue china, children, I shan't care or
    ho.'

All. – 'We've no wish to hear the tidings, how the people's fortunes
    shift;
—   What your daily doings are;
    Who are wedded, born, divided; if your lives beat slow or swift.

'Curious not the least are we if our intents you make or mar,
    If you quire to our old tune,
If the City stage still passes, if the weirs still roar afar.'

– Thus, with very gods' composure, freed those crosses late and soon
    Which, in life, the Trine allow
(Why, none witteth), and ignoring all that haps beneath the moon,

William Dewy, Tranter Reuben, Farmer Ledlow late at plough,
    Robert's kin, and John's, and Ned's,
And the Squire, and Lady Susan, murmur mildly to me now.

38 Thoughts of Phena

At News of Her Death

NOT a line of her writing have I,
    Not a thread of her hair,
No mark of her late time as dame in her dwelling, whereby
    I may picture her there;
    And in vain do I urge my unsight
    To conceive my lost prize
At her close, whom I knew when her dreams were upbrimming
    with light,
    And with laughter her eyes.

    What scenes spread around her last days,
    Sad, shining, or dim?
Did her gifts and compassions enray and enarch her sweet ways
    With an aureate nimb?
    Or did life-light decline from her years,
    And mischances control
Her full day-star; unease, or regret, or forebodings, or fears
    Disennoble her soul?

    Thus I do but the phantom retain
    Of the maiden of yore
As my relic; yet haply the best of her – fined in my brain
    It may be the more
    That no line of her writing have I,
    Nor a thread of her hair,
No mark of her late time as dame in her dwelling, whereby
    I may picture her there.

March 1890

To M.H.

WE passed where flag and flower
Signalled a jocund throng;
We said: 'Go to, the hour
Is apt!' – and joined the song;
And, kindling, laughed at life and care,
Although we knew no laugh lay there.

We walked where shy birds stood
Watching us, wonder-dumb;
Their friendship met our mood;
We cried: 'We'll often come:
We'll come morn, noon, eve, everywhen!'
– We doubted we should come again.

We joyed to see strange sheens
Leap from quaint leaves in shade;
A secret light of greens
They'd for their pleasure made.
We said: 'We'll set such sorts as these!'
– We knew with night the wish would cease.

'So sweet the place,' we said,
'Its tacit tales so dear,
Our thoughts, when breath has sped,
Will meet and mingle here!' . . .
'Words!' mused we. 'Passed the mortal door,
Our thoughts will reach this nook no more.'

40 In a Wood

See 'The Woodlanders'

PALE beech and pine so blue,
    Set in one clay,
Bough to bough cannot you
    Live out your day?
When the rains skim and skip,
Why mar sweet comradeship,
Blighting with poison-drip
    Neighbourly spray?

Heart-halt and spirit-lame,
    City-opprest,
Unto this wood I came
    As to a nest;
Dreaming that sylvan peace
Offered the harrowed ease –
Nature a soft release
    From men's unrest.

But, having entered in,
    Great growths and small
Show them to men akin –
    Combatants all!
Sycamore shoulders oak,
Bines the slim sapling yoke,
Ivy-spun halters choke
    Elms stout and tall.

Touches from ash, O wych,
    Sting you like scorn!
You, too, brave hollies, twitch
    Sidelong from thorn.
Even the rank poplars bear
Lothly a rival's air,
Cankering in black despair
    If overborne.

Since, then, no grace I find
    Taught me of trees,

Turn I back to my kind,
      Worthy as these.
There at least smiles abound,
There discourse trills around,
There, now and then, are found
      Life-loyalties.

   1887: 1896

43 *Nature's Questioning*

WHEN I look forth at dawning, pool,
      Field, flock, and lonely tree,
      All seem to gaze at me
Like chastened children sitting silent in a school;

   Their faces dulled, constrained, and worn,
      As though the master's ways
      Through the long teaching days
Had cowed them till their early zest was overborne.

   Upon them stirs in lippings mere
      (As if once clear in call,
      But now scarce breathed at all) –
'We wonder, ever wonder, why we find us here!

   'Has some Vast Imbecility,
      Mighty to build and blend,
      But impotent to tend,
Framed us in jest, and left us now to hazardry?

   'Or come we of an Automaton
      Unconscious of our pains? . . .
      Or are we live remains
Of Godhead dying downwards, brain and eye now gone?

   'Or is it that some high Plan betides,
      As yet not understood,

Of Evil stormed by Good,
We the Forlorn Hope over which Achievement strides?'

Thus things around. No answerer I. . . .
Meanwhile the winds, and rains,
And Earth's old glooms and pains
Are still the same, and Life and Death are neighbours nigh.

44 *The Impercipient*

(*At a Cathedral Service*)

THAT with this bright believing band
I have no claim to be,
That faiths by which my comrades stand
Seem fantasies to me,
And mirage-mists their Shining Land,
Is a strange destiny.

Why thus my soul should be consigned
To infelicity,
Why always I must feel as blind
To sights my brethren see,
Why joys they've found I cannot find,
Abides a mystery.

Since heart of mine knows not that ease
Which they know; since it be
That He who breathes All's Well to these
Breathes no All's-Well to me,
My lack might move their sympathies
And Christian charity!

I am like a gazer who should mark
An inland company
Standing upfingered, with, 'Hark! hark!
The glorious distant sea!'
And feel, 'Alas, 'tis but yon dark
And wind-swept pine to me!'

Yet I would bear my shortcomings
　　With meet tranquillity,
But for the charge that blessed things
　　I'd liefer not have be.
O, doth a bird deprived of wings
　　Go earth-bound wilfully!

　　　　．　　　　．　　　　．

Enough. As yet disquiet clings
　　About us. Rest shall we.

47 *In a Eweleaze near Weatherbury*

THE years have gathered grayly
　　Since I danced upon this leaze
With one who kindled gaily
　　Love's fitful ecstasies!
But despite the term as teacher,
　　I remain what I was then
In each essential feature
　　Of the fantasies of men.

Yet I note the little chisel
　　Of never-napping Time
Defacing wan and grizzel
　　The blazon of my prime.
When at night he thinks me sleeping
　　I feel him boring sly
Within my bones, and heaping
　　Quaintest pains for by-and-by.

Still, I'd go the world with Beauty,
　　I would laugh with her and sing,
I would shun divinest duty
　　To resume her worshipping.
But she'd scorn my brave endeavour,
　　She would not balm the breeze
By murmuring 'Thine for ever!'
　　As she did upon this leaze.

1890

48 The Bride-Night Fire

(A Wessex Tradition)

THEY had long met o' Zundays – her true love and she –
   And at junketings, maypoles, and flings;
But she bode wi' a thirtover[1] uncle, and he
Swore by noon and by night that her goodman should be
Naibour Sweatley – a wight often weak at the knee
From taking o' sommat more cheerful than tea –
   Who tranted,[2] and moved people's things.

She cried, 'O pray pity me!' Nought would he hear;
   Then with wild rainy eyes she obeyed.
She chid when her Love was for clinking off wi' her:
The pa'son was told, as the season drew near,
To throw over pu'pit the names of the pair
   As fitting one flesh to be made.

The wedding-day dawned and the morning drew on;
   The couple stood bridegroom and bride;
The evening was passed, and when midnight had gone
The feasters horned,[3] 'God save the King,' and anon
   The pair took their homealong[4] ride.

The lover Tim Tankens mourned heart-sick and leer[5]
   To be thus of his darling deprived:
He roamed in the dark ath'art field, mound, and mere,
And, a'most without knowing it, found himself near
The house of the tranter, and now of his Dear,
   Where the lantern-light showed 'em arrived.

The bride sought her chamber so calm and so pale
   That a Northern had thought her resigned;
But to eyes that had seen her in tidetimes[6] of weal,
Like the white cloud o' smoke, the red battlefield's vail,
   That look spak' of havoc behind.

[1] *thirtover*, cross   [2] *tranted*, traded as carrier
[3] *horned*, sang loudly   [4] *homealong*, homeward
[5] *leer*, empty-stomached   [6] *tidetimes*, holidays

The bridegroom yet laitered a beaker to drain,
   Then reeled to the linhay[1] for more,
When the candle-snoff kindled some chaff from his grain –
Flames spread, and red vlankers[2] wi' might and wi' main
   Around beams, thatch, and chimley-tun[3] roar.

Young Tim away yond, rafted[4] up by the light,
   Through brimbles and underwood tears,
Till he comes to the orchet, when crooping[5] from sight
In the lewth[6] of a codlin-tree, bivering[7] wi' fright,
Wi' on'y her night-rail to cover her plight,
   His lonesome young Barbree appears.

Her cwold little figure half-naked he views
   Played about by the frolicsome breeze,
Her light-tripping totties[8] her ten little tooes,
All bare and besprinkled wi' Fall's[9] chilly dews,
While her great gallied[10] eyes through her hair hanging loose
   Shone as stars through a tardle[11] o' trees.

She eyed him; and, as when a weir-hatch is drawn,
   Her tears, penned by terror afore,
With a rushing of sobs in a shower were strawn,
Till her power to pour 'em seemed wasted and gone
   From the heft[12] o' misfortune she bore.

'O Tim, my *own* Tim I must call 'ee – I will!
   All the world has turned round on me so!
Can you help her who loved 'ee, though acting so ill?
Can you pity her misery – feel for her still?
When worse than her body so quivering and chill
   Is her heart in its winter o' woe!

'I think I mid[13] almost ha' borne it,' she said,
   'Had my griefs one by one come to hand;
But O, to be slave to thik husbird,[14] for bread,

---

[1] *linhay*, lean-to building   [2] *vlankers*, fire-flakes
[3] *chimley-tun*, chimney-stack   [4] *rafted*, roused
[5] *crooping*, squatting down   [6] *lewth*, shelter
[7] *bivering*, with chattering teeth   [8] *totties*, feet
[9] *Fall*, autumn   [10] *gallied*, frightened
[11] *tardle*, entanglement   [12] *heft*, weight
[13] *mid*, might   [14] *thik husbird*, that rascal

And then, upon top o' that, driven to wed,
And then, upon top o' that, burnt out o' bed,
  Is more than my nater can stand!'

Like a lion 'ithin en Tim's spirit outsprung –
(Tim had a great soul when his feelings were wrung) –
  'Feel for 'ee, dear Barbree?' he cried;
And his warm working-jacket then straightway he flung
Round about her, and horsed her by jerks, till she clung
Like a chiel on a gipsy, her figure uphung
  By the sleeves that he tightly had tied.

Over piggeries, and mixens,[1] and apples, and hay,
  They lumpered[2] straight into the night;
And finding ere long where a halter-path[3] lay,
Sighted Tim's house by dawn, on'y seen on their way
By a naibour or two who were up wi' the day,
  But who gathered no clue to the sight.

Then tender Tim Tankens he searched here and there
  For some garment to clothe her fair skin;
But though he had breeches and waistcoats to spare,
He had nothing quite seemly for Barbree to wear,
Who, half shrammed[4] to death, stood and cried on a chair
  At the caddle[5] she found herself in.

There was one thing to do, and that one thing he did,
  He lent her some clothes of his own,
And she took 'em perforce; and while swiftly she slid
Them upon her Tim turned to the winder, as bid,
Thinking, 'O that the picter my duty keeps hid
  To the sight o' my eyes mid[6] be shown!'

In the tallet[7] he stowed her; there huddied[8] she lay,
  Shortening sleeves, legs, and tails to her limbs;
But most o' the time in a mortal bad way,
Well knowing that there'd be the divel to pay
If 'twere found that, instead o' the element's prey,
  She was living in lodgings at Tim's.

---

[1] *mixens*, manure-heaps   [2] *lumpered*, stumbled   [3] *halter-path*, bridle-path
[4] *shrammed*, numbed   [5] *caddle*, quandary   [6] *mid*, might   [7] *tallet*, loft
[8] *huddied*, hidden

'Where's the tranter?' said men and boys; 'where can he be?'
  'Where's the tranter?' said Barbree alone.
'Where on e'th is the tranter?' said everybod-y:
They sifted the dust of his perished roof-tree,
  And all they could find was a bone.

Then the uncle cried, 'Lord, pray have mercy on me!'
  And in terror began to repent.
But before 'twas complete, and till sure she was free,
Barbree drew up her loft-ladder, tight turned her key –
Tim bringing up breakfast and dinner and tea –
  Till the news of her hiding got vent.

Then followed the custom-kept rout, shout, and flare
Of a skimmity-ride[1] through the naibourhood, ere
  Folk had proof o' wold[2] Sweatley's decay.
Whereupon decent people all stood in a stare,
Saying Tim and his lodger should risk it, and pair:
So he took her to church. An' some laughing lads there
Cried to Tim, 'After Sweatley!' She said, 'I declare
  I stand as a maiden to-day!'

  Written 1866; printed 1875

[1] *skimmity-ride*, satirical procession with effigies   [2] *wold*, old

I LOOK into my glass,
And view my wasting skin,
And say, 'Would God it came to pass
My heart had shrunk as thin!'

For then, I, undistrest
By hearts grown cold to me,
Could lonely wait my endless rest
With equanimity.

But Time, to make me grieve,
Part steals, lets part abide;
And shakes this fragile frame at eve
With throbbings of noontide.

60 *Drummer Hodge*

I

THEY throw in Drummer Hodge, to rest
    Uncoffined – just as found:
His landmark is a kopje-crest
    That breaks the veldt around;
And foreign constellations west
    Each night above his mound.

II

Young Hodge the Drummer never knew –
    Fresh from his Wessex home –
The meaning of the broad Karoo,
    The Bush, the dusty loam,
And why uprose to nightly view
    Strange stars amid the gloam.

III

Yet portion of that unknown plain
    Will Hodge for ever be;

His homely Northern breast and brain
  Grow to some Southern tree,
And strange-eyed constellations reign
  His stars eternally.

66 *Shelley's Skylark*

(The neighbourhood of Leghorn: March 1887)

SOMEWHERE afield here something lies
In Earth's oblivious eyeless trust
That moved a poet to prophecies –
A pinch of unseen, unguarded dust:

The dust of the lark that Shelley heard,
And made immortal through times to be; –
Though it only lived like another bird,
And knew not its immortality:

Lived its meek life; then, one day, fell –
A little ball of feather and bone;
And how it perished, when piped farewell,
And where it wastes, are alike unknown.

Maybe it rests in the loam I view,
Maybe it throbs in a myrtle's green,
Maybe it sleeps in the coming hue
Of a grape on the slopes of yon inland scene.

Go find it, faeries, go and find
That tiny pinch of priceless dust,
And bring a casket silver-lined,
And framed of gold that gems encrust;

And we will lay it safe therein,
And consecrate it to endless time;
For it inspired a bard to win
Ecstatic heights in thought and rhyme.

69 Rome
Building a New Street in the Ancient Quarter

(April 1887)

THESE umbered cliffs and gnarls of masonry
Outskeleton Time's central city, Rome;
Whereof each arch, entablature, and dome
Lies bare in all its gaunt anatomy.

And cracking frieze and rotten metope
Express, as though they were an open tome
Top-lined with caustic monitory gnome;
'Dunces, Learn here to spell Humanity!'

And yet within these ruins' very shade
The singing workmen shape and set and join
Their frail new mansion's stuccoed cove and quoin
With no apparent sense that years abrade,
Though each rent wall their feeble works invade
Once shamed all such in power of pier and groin.

71 Rome
At the Pyramid of Cestius near the Graves of Shelley and Keats

(1887)

WHO, then, was Cestius,
And what is he to me? –
Amid thick thoughts and memories multitudinous
One thought alone brings he.

I can recall no word
Of anything he did;
For me he is a man who died and was interred
To leave a pyramid

52

Whose purpose was exprest
Not with its first design,
Nor till, far down in Time, beside it found their rest
Two countrymen of mine.

Cestius in life, maybe,
Slew, breathed out threatening;
I know not. This I know: in death all silently
He does a finer thing,

In beckoning pilgrim feet
With marble finger high
To where, by shadowy wall and history-haunted street,
Those matchless singers lie. . . .

– Say, then, he lived and died
That stones which bear his name
Should mark, through Time, where two immortal Shades abide;
It is an ample fame.

79 *At a Lunar Eclipse*

THY shadow, Earth, from Pole to Central Sea,
Now steals along upon the Moon's meek shine
In even monochrome and curving line
Of imperturbable serenity.

How shall I link such sun-cast symmetry
With the torn troubled form I know as thine,
That profile, placid as a brow divine,
With continents of moil and misery?

And can immense Mortality but throw
So small a shade, and Heaven's high human scheme
Be hemmed within the coasts yon arc implies?

Is such the stellar gauge of earthly show,
Nation at war with nation, brains that teem,
Heroes, and women fairer than the skies?

I

BREATHE not, hid Heart: cease silently,
And though thy birth-hour beckons thee,
 Sleep the long sleep:
 The Doomsters heap
Travails and teens around us here,
And Time-wraiths turn our songsingings to fear.

II

Hark, how the peoples surge and sigh,
And laughters fail, and greetings die:
 Hopes dwindle; yea,
 Faiths waste away,
Affections and enthusiasms numb;
Thou canst not mend these things if thou dost come.

III

Had I the ear of wombèd souls
Ere their terrestrial chart unrolls,
 And thou wert free
 To cease, or be,
Then would I tell thee all I know,
And put it to thee: Wilt thou take Life so?

IV

Vain vow! No hint of mine may hence
To theeward fly: to thy locked sense
 Explain none can
 Life's pending plan:
Thou wilt thy ignorant entry make
Though skies spout fire and blood and nations quake.

V

Fain would I, dear, find some shut plot
Of earth's wide wold for thee, where not
 One tear, one qualm,
 Should break the calm.
But I am weak as thou and bare;
No man can change the common lot to rare.

Must come and bide. And such are we –
Unreasoning, sanguine, visionary –
    That I can hope
    Health, love, friends, scope
In full for thee; can dream thou'lt find
Joys seldom yet attained by humankind!

94 *To Lizbie Browne*

I

Dear Lizbie Browne,
Where are you now?
In sun, in rain? –
Or is your brow
Past joy, past pain,
Dear Lizbie Browne?

II

Sweet Lizbie Browne,
How you could smile,
How you could sing! –
How archly wile
In glance-giving,
Sweet Lizbie Browne!

III

And, Lizbie Browne,
Who else had hair
Bay-red as yours,
Or flesh so fair
Bred out of doors,
Sweet Lizbie Browne?

IV

When, Lizbie Browne,
You had just begun
To be endeared
By stealth to one,
You disappeared
My Lizbie Browne!

V

Ay, Lizbie Browne,
So swift your life,
And mine so slow,
You were a wife
Ere I could show
Love, Lizbie Browne.

VI

Still, Lizbie Browne,
You won, they said,
The best of men
When you were wed. . . .
Where went you then,
O Lizbie Browne?

VII

Dear Lizbie Browne,
I should have thought,
'Girls ripen fast,'
And coaxed and caught
You ere you passed,
Dear Lizbie Browne!

VIII

But, Lizbie Browne,
I let you slip;
Shaped not a sign;
Touched never your lip
With lip of mine,
Lost Lizbie Browne!

I

Never a careworn wife but shows,
　　If a joy suffuse her,
Something beautiful to those
　　Patient to peruse her,
Some one charm the world unknows
　　Precious to a muser,
Haply what, ere years were foes,
　　Moved her mate to choose her.

II

But, be it a hint of rose
　　That an instant hues her,
Or some early light or pose
　　Wherewith thought renews her –
Seen by him at full, ere woes
　　Practised to abuse her –
Sparely comes it, swiftly goes,
　　Time again subdues her.

113 *An August Midnight*

I

A SHADED lamp and a waving blind,
And the beat of a clock from a distant floor:
On this scene enter – winged, horned, and spined –
A longlegs, a moth, and a dumbledore;
While 'mid my page there idly stands
A sleepy fly, that rubs its hands. . . .

II

Thus meet we five, in this still place,
At this point of time, at this point in space.
– My guests besmear my new-penned line,
Or bang at the lamp and fall supine.
'God's humblest, they!' I muse. Yet why?
They know Earth-secrets that know not I.

Max Gate, 1899

116 *The Puzzled Game-Birds*

(*Triolet*)

THEY are not those who used to feed us
When we were young – they cannot be –
These shapes that now bereave and bleed us?
They are not those who used to feed us,
For did we then cry, they would heed us.
– If hearts can house such treachery
They are not those who used to feed us
When we were young – they cannot be!

WHY should this flower delay so long
    To show its tremulous plumes?
Now is the time of plaintive robin-song,
    When flowers are in their tombs.

Through the slow summer, when the sun
    Called to each frond and whorl
That all he could for flowers was being done,
    Why did it not uncurl?

It must have felt that fervid call
    Although it took no heed,
Waking but now, when leaves like corpses fall,
    And saps all retrocede.

Too late its beauty, lonely thing,
    The season's shine is spent,
Nothing remains for it but shivering
    In tempests turbulent.

Had it a reason for delay,
    Dreaming in witlessness
That for a bloom so delicately gay
    Winter would stay its stress?

– I talk as if the thing were born
    With sense to work its mind;
Yet it is but one mask of many worn
    By the Great Face behind.

I LEANT upon a coppice gate
    When Frost was spectre-gray,
And Winter's dregs made desolate
    The weakening eye of day.
The tangled bine-stems scored the sky
    Like strings of broken lyres,
And all mankind that haunted nigh
    Had sought their household fires.

The land's sharp features seemed to be
    The Century's corpse outleant,
His crypt the cloudy canopy,
    The wind his death-lament.
The ancient pulse of germ and birth
    Was shrunken hard and dry,
And every spirit upon earth
    Seemed fervourless as I.

At once a voice arose among
    The bleak twigs overhead
In a full-hearted evensong
    Of joy illimited;
An aged thrush, frail, gaunt, and small,
    In blast-beruffled plume,
Had chosen thus to fling his soul
    Upon the growing gloom.

So little cause for carolings
    Of such ecstatic sound
Was written on terrestrial things
    Afar or nigh around,
That I could think there trembled through
    His happy good-night air
Some blessed Hope, whereof he knew
    And I was unaware.

31 December 1900

WHEN the hamlet hailed a birth
   Judy used to cry:
When she heard our christening mirth
   She would kneel and sigh.
She was crazed, we knew, and we
Humoured her infirmity.

When the daughters and the sons
   Gathered them to wed,
And we like-intending ones
   Danced till dawn was red,
She would rock and mutter, 'More
Comers to this stony shore!'

When old Headsman Death laid hands
   On a babe or twain,
She would feast, and by her brands
   Sing her songs again.
What she liked we let her do,
Judy was insane, we knew.

'O PASSENGER, pray list and catch
        Our sighs and piteous groans,
Half stifled in this jumbled patch
        Of wrenched memorial stones!

'We late-lamented, resting here,
        Are mixed to human jam,
And each to each exclaims in fear,
        "I know not which I am!"

'The wicked people have annexed
        The verses on the good;
A roaring drunkard sports the text
        Teetotal Tommy should!

'Where we are huddled none can trace,
        And if our names remain,
They pave some path or porch or place
        Where we have never lain!

'Here's not a modest maiden elf
        But dreads the final Trumpet,
Lest half of her should rise herself,
        And half some sturdy strumpet!

'From restorations of Thy fane,
        From smoothings of Thy sward,
From zealous Churchmen's pick and plane
        Deliver us O Lord! Amen!'

1882

'O 'MELIA, my dear, this does everything crown!
Who could have supposed I should meet you in Town?
And whence such fair garments, such prosperi-ty?' –
'O didn't you know I'd been ruined?' said she.

– 'You left us in tatters, without shoes or socks,
Tired of digging potatoes, and spudding up docks;
And now you've gay bracelets and bright feathers three!' –
'Yes: that's how we dress when we're ruined,' said she.

– 'At home in the barton you said "thee" and "thou",
And "thik oon", and "theäs oon", and "t'other"; but now
Your talking quite fits 'ee for high compa-ny!' –
'Some polish is gained with one's ruin,' said she.

– 'Your hands were like paws then, your face blue and bleak
But now I'm bewitched by your delicate cheek,
And your little gloves fit as on any la-dy!' –
'We never do work when we're ruined,' said she.

– 'You used to call home-life a hag-ridden dream,
And you'd sigh, and you'd sock; but at present you seem
To know not of megrims or melancho-ly!' –
'True. One's pretty lively when ruined,' said she.

– 'I wish I had feathers, a fine sweeping gown,
And a delicate face, and could strut about Town!' –
'My dear – a raw country girl, such as you be,
Cannot quite expect that. You ain't ruined,' said she.

Westbourne Park Villas, 1866

I

THERE is a house with ivied walls,
And mullioned windows worn and old,
And the long dwellers in those halls
Have souls that know but sordid calls,
  And daily dote on gold.

II

In blazing brick and plated show
Not far away a 'villa' gleams,
And here a family few may know,
With book and pencil, viol and bow,
  Lead inner lives of dreams.

III

The philosophic passers say,
'See that old mansion mossed and fair,
Poetic souls therein are they:
And O that gaudy box! Away,
  You vulgar people there.'

135 *The Self-Unseeing*

HERE is the ancient floor,
Footworn and hollowed and thin,
Here was the former door
Where the dead feet walked in.

She sat here in her chair,
Smiling into the fire;
He who played stood there,
Bowing it higher and higher.

Childlike, I danced in a dream;
Blessings emblazoned that day;
Everything glowed with a gleam;
Yet we were looking away!

136 *In Tenebris* I

'Percussus sum sicut fœnum, et aruit cor meum.' – Ps. CI

WINTERTIME nighs;
But my bereavement-pain
It cannot bring again:
  Twice no one dies.

  Flower-petals flee;
But, since it once hath been,
No more that severing scene
  Can harrow me.

  Birds faint in dread:
I shall not lose old strength
In the lone frost's black length:
  Strength long since fled!

  Leaves freeze to dun;
But friends can not turn cold
This season as of old
  For him with none.

Tempests may scath;
But love can not make smart
Again this year his heart
　　Who no heart hath.

　　Black is night's cope;
But death will not appal
One who, past doubtings all,
　　Waits in unhope.

140 *The Lost Pyx*

A Mediæval Legend [1]

SOME say the spot is banned: that the pillar Cross-and-Hand
　　Attests to a deed of hell;
But of else than of bale is the mystic tale
　　That ancient Vale-folk tell.

Ere Cernel's Abbey ceased hereabout there dwelt a priest,
　　(In later life sub-prior
Of the brotherhood there, whose bones are now bare
　　In the field that was Cernel choir).

One night in his cell at the foot of yon dell
　　The priest heard a frequent cry:
'Go, father, in haste to the cot on the waste,
　　And shrive a man waiting to die.'

Said the priest in a shout to the caller without,
　　'The night howls, the tree-trunks bow;
One may barely by day track so rugged a way,
　　And can I then do so now?'

---

[1] On a lonely table-land above the Vale of Blackmore, between
High-Stoy and Bubb-Down hills, and commanding in clear weather
views that extend from the English to the Bristol Channel, stands a
pillar, apparently mediæval, called Cross-and-Hand, or Christ-in-
Hand. One tradition of its origin is mentioned in *Tess of the d'Urber-
villes*; another, more detailed, preserves the story here given.

No further word from the dark was heard,
    And the priest moved never a limb;
And he slept and dreamed; till a Visage seemed
    To frown from Heaven at him.

In a sweat he arose; and the storm shrieked shrill,
    And smote as in savage joy;
While High-Stoy trees twanged to Bubb-Down Hill,
    And Bubb-Down to High-Stoy.

There seemed not a holy thing in hail,
    Nor shape of light or love,
From the Abbey north of Blackmore Vale
    To the Abbey south thereof.

Yet he plodded thence through the dark immense,
    And with many a stumbling stride
Through copse and briar climbed nigh and nigher
    To the cot and the sick man's side.

When he would have unslung the Vessels uphung
    To his arm in the steep ascent,
He made loud moan: the Pyx was gone
    Of the Blessed Sacrament.

Then in dolorous dread he beat his head:
    'No earthly prize or pelf
Is the thing I've lost in tempest tossed,
    But the Body of Christ Himself!'

He thought of the Visage his dream revealed,
    And turned towards whence he came,
Hands groping the ground along foot-track and field,
    And head in a heat of shame.

Till here on the hill, betwixt vill and vill,
    He noted a clear straight ray
Stretching down from the sky to a spot hard by,
    Which shone with the light of day.

And gathered around the illumined ground
    Were common beasts and rare,

All kneeling at gaze, and in pause profound
    Attent on an object there.

'Twas the Pyx, unharmed 'mid the circling rows
    Of Blackmore's hairy throng,
Whereof were oxen, sheep, and does,
    And hares from the brakes among;

And badgers grey, and conies keen,
    And squirrels of the tree,
And many a member seldom seen
    Of Nature's family.

The ireful winds that scoured and swept
    Through coppice, clump, and dell,
Within that holy circle slept
    Calm as in hermit's cell.

Then the priest bent likewise to the sod
    And thanked the Lord of Love,
And Blessed Mary, Mother of God,
    And all the saints above.

And turning straight with his priceless freight,
    He reached the dying one,
Whose passing sprite had been stayed for the rite
    Without which bliss hath none.

And when by grace the priest won place,
    And served the Abbey well,
He reared this stone to mark where shone
    That midnight miracle.

148 Cardinal Bembo's Epitaph on Raphael

HERE'S one in whom Nature feared – faint at such vying –
Eclipse while he lived, and decease at his dying.

156 The House of Hospitalities

HERE we broached the Christmas barrel,
    Pushed up the charred log-ends;
Here we sang the Christmas carol,
    And called in friends.

Time has tired me since we met here
    When the folk now dead were young,
Since the viands were outset here
    And quaint songs sung.

And the worm has bored the viol
    That used to lead the tune,
Rust eaten out the dial
    That struck night's noon.

Now no Christmas brings in neighbours,
    And the New Year comes unlit;
Where we sang the mole now labours,
    And spiders knit.

Yet at midnight if here walking,
    When the moon sheets wall and tree,
I see forms of old time talking,
    Who smile on me.

HERE by the baring bough
　　Raking up leaves,
Often I ponder how
　　Springtime deceives, –
I, an old woman now,
　　Raking up leaves.

Here in the avenue
　　Raking up leaves,
Lords' ladies pass in view,
　　Until one heaves
Sighs at life's russet hue,
　　Raking up leaves!

Just as my shape you see
　　Raking up leaves,
I saw, when fresh and free,
　　Those memory weaves
Into grey ghosts by me,
　　Raking up leaves.

Yet, Dear, though one may sigh,
　　Raking up leaves,
New leaves will dance on high –
　　Earth never grieves! –
Will not, when missed am I
　　Raking up leaves.

1901

CLOSE up the casement, draw the blind,
    Shut out that stealing moon,
She wears too much the guise she wore
    Before our lutes were strewn
With years-deep dust, and names we read
    On a white stone were hewn.

Step not forth on the dew-dashed lawn
    To view the Lady's Chair,
Immense Orion's glittering form,
    The Less and Greater Bear:
Stay in; to such sights we were drawn
    When faded ones were fair.

Brush not the bough for midnight scents
    That come forth lingeringly,
And wake the same sweet sentiments
    They breathed to you and me
When living seemed a laugh, and love
    All it was said to be.

Within the common lamp-lit room
    Prison my eyes and thought;
Let dingy details crudely loom,
    Mechanic speech be wrought:
Too fragrant was Life's early bloom,
    Too tart the fruit it brought!

1904

INDULGE no more may we
In this sweet-bitter pastime:
The love-light shines the last time
   Between you, Dear, and me.

There shall remain no trace
Of what so closely tied us,
And blank as ere love eyed us
   Will be our meeting-place.

The flowers and thymy air,
Will they now miss our coming?
The dumbles thin their humming
   To find we haunt not there?

Though fervent was our vow,
Though ruddily ran our pleasure,
Bliss has fulfilled its measure,
   And sees its sentence now.

Ache deep; but make no moans:
Smile out; but stilly suffer:
The paths of love are rougher
   Than thoroughfares of stones.

THE cold moon hangs to the sky by its horn,
    And centres its gaze on me;
The stars, like eyes in reverie,
Their westering as for a while forborne,
    Quiz downward curiously.

Old Robert draws the backbrand in,
    The green logs steam and spit;
The half-awakened sparrows flit
From the riddled thatch; and owls begin
    To whoo from the gable-slit.

Yes; far and nigh things seem to know
    Sweet scenes are impending here;
That all is prepared; that the hour is near
For welcomes, fellowships, and flow
    Of sally, song, and cheer;

That spigots are pulled and viols strung;
    That soon will arise the sound
Of measures trod to tunes renowned;
That She will return in Love's low tongue
    My vows as we wheel around.

193 Let Me Enjoy

I

Let me enjoy the earth no less
Because the all-enacting Might
That fashioned forth its loveliness
Had other aims than my delight.

II

About my path there flits a Fair,
Who throws me not a word or sign;
I'll charm me with her ignoring air,
And laud the lips not meant for mine.

III

From manuscripts of moving song
Inspired by scenes and dreams unknown
I'll pour out raptures that belong
To others, as they were my own.

IV

And some day hence, towards Paradise
And all its blest – if such should be –
I will lift glad, afar-off eyes,
Though it contain no place for me.

At Casterbridge Fair

195 II. Former Beauties

THESE market-dames, mid-aged, with lips thin-drawn,
    And tissues sere,
Are they the ones we loved in years agone,
    And courted here?

Are these the muslined pink young things to whom
    We vowed and swore
In nooks on summer Sundays by the Froom,
    Or Budmouth shore?

Do they remember those gay tunes we trod
    Clasped on the green;
Aye; trod till moonlight set on the beaten sod
    A satin sheen?

They must forget, forget! They cannot know
    What once they were,
Or memory would transfigure them, and show
    Them always fair.

211 A Church Romance

(Mellstock: circa 1835)

SHE turned in the high pew, until her sight
Swept the west gallery, and caught its row
Of music-men with viol, book, and bow
Against the sinking sad tower-window light.

She turned again; and in her pride's despite
One strenuous viol's inspirer seemed to throw
A message from his string to her below,
Which said: 'I claim thee as my own forthright!'

Thus their hearts' bond began, in due time signed.
And long years thence, when Age had scared Romance,
At some old attitude of his or glance
That gallery-scene would break upon her mind,
With him as minstrel, ardent, young, and trim,
Bowing 'New Sabbath' or 'Mount Ephraim'.

218 The Roman Road

THE Roman Road runs straight and bare
As the pale parting-line in hair
Across the heath. And thoughtful men
Contrast its days of Now and Then,
And delve, and measure, and compare;

Visioning on the vacant air
Helmed legionaries, who proudly rear
The Eagle, as they pace again
         The Roman Road.

But no tall brass-helmed legionnaire
Haunts it for me. Uprises there
A mother's form upon my ken,
Guiding my infant steps, as when
We walked that ancient thoroughfare,
         The Roman Road.

227 One We Knew

(M.H. 1772–1857)

SHE told how they used to form for the country dances –
    'The Triumph', 'The New-rigged Ship' –
To the light of the guttering wax in the panelled manses,
    And in cots to the blink of a dip.

She spoke of the wild 'poussetting' and 'allemanding'
    On carpet, on oak, and on sod;
And the two long rows of ladies and gentlemen standing,
    And the figures the couples trod.

She showed us the spot where the maypole was yearly planted,
    And where the bandsmen stood
While breeched and kerchiefed partners whirled, and panted
    To choose each other for good.

She told of that far-back day when they learnt astounded
    Of the death of the King of France:
Of the Terror; and then of Bonaparte's unbounded
    Ambition and arrogance.

Of how his threats woke warlike preparations
    Along the southern strand,
And how each night brought tremors and trepidations
    Lest morning should see him land.

She said she had often heard the gibbet creaking
    As it swayed in the lightning flash,
Had caught from the neighbouring town a small child's shrieking
    At the cart-tail under the lash. . . .

With cap-framed face and long gaze into the embers –
    We seated around her knees –
She would dwell on such dead themes, not as one who remembers,
    But rather as one who sees.

She seemed one left behind of a band gone distant
    So far that no tongue could hail:
Past things retold were to her as things existent,
    Things present but as a tale.

20 May 1902

THERE was a time in former years –
　　While my roof-tree was his –
When I should have been distressed by fears
　　At such a night as this!

I should have murmured anxiously,
　　'The pricking rain strikes cold;
His road is bare of hedge or tree,
　　And he is getting old.'

But now the fitful chimney-roar,
　　The drone of Thorncombe trees,
The Froom in flood upon the moor,
　　The mud of Mellstock Leaze,

The candle slanting sooty-wick'd,
　　The thuds upon the thatch,
The eaves-drops on the window flicked,
　　The clacking garden-hatch,

And what they mean to wayfarers,
　　I scarcely heed or mind;
He has won that storm-tight roof of hers
　　Which Earth grants all her kind.

I ROSE at night, and visited
    The Cave of the Unborn:
And crowding shapes surrounded me
For tidings of the life to be,
Who long had prayed the silent Head
    To haste its advent morn.

Their eyes were lit with artless trust,
    Hope thrilled their every tone;
'A scene the loveliest, is it not?
A pure delight, a beauty-spot
Where all is gentle, true and just,
    And darkness is unknown?'

My heart was anguished for their sake,
    I could not frame a word;
And they descried my sunken face,
And seemed to read therein, and trace
The news that pity would not break,
    Nor truth leave unaverred.

And as I silently retired
    I turned and watched them still,
And they came helter-skelter out,
Driven forward like a rabble rout
Into the world they had so desired,
    By the all-immanent Will.

1905

'HAD he and I but met
By some old ancient inn,
We should have sat us down to wet
Right many a nipperkin!

'But ranged as infantry,
And staring face to face,
I shot at him as he at me,
And killed him in his place.

'I shot him dead because –
Because he was my foe,
Just so: my foe of course he was;
That's clear enough; although

'He thought he'd 'list, perhaps,
Off-hand like – just as I –
Was out of work – had sold his traps –
No other reason why.

'Yes; quaint and curious war is!
You shoot a fellow down
You'd treat if met where any bar is,
Or help to half-a-crown.'

1902

243 George Meredith

(1828–1909)

FORTY years back, when much had place
That since has perished out of mind,
I heard that voice and saw that face.

He spoke as one afoot will wind
A morning horn ere men awake;
His note was trenchant, turning kind.

He was of those whose wit can shake
And riddle to the very core
The counterfeits that Time will break. . . .

Of late, when we two met once more,
The luminous countenance and rare
Shone just as forty years before.

So that, when now all tongues declare
His shape unseen by his green hill,
I scarce believe he sits not there.

No matter. Further and further still
Through the world's vaporous vitiate air
His words wing on – as live words will.

May 1909

THAT night your great guns, unawares,
Shook all our coffins as we lay,
And broke the chancel window-squares,
We thought it was the Judgment-day

And sat upright. While drearisome
Arose the howl of wakened hounds:
The mouse let fall the altar-crumb,
The worms drew back into the mounds,

The glebe cow drooled. Till God called, 'No;
It's gunnery practice out at sea
Just as before you went below;
The world is as it used to be:

'All nations striving strong to make
Red war yet redder. Mad as hatters
They do no more for Christés sake
Than you who are helpless in such matters.

'That this is not the judgment-hour
For some of them's a blessed thing,
For if it were they'd have to scour
Hell's floor for so much threatening. . . .

'Ha, ha. It will be warmer when
I blow the trumpet (if indeed
I ever do; for you are men,
And rest eternal sorely need).'

So down we lay again. 'I wonder,
Will the world ever saner be,'
Said one, 'than when He sent us under
In our indifferent century!'

And many a skeleton shook his head.
'Instead of preaching forty year,'
My neighbour Parson Thirdly said,
'I wish I had stuck to pipes and beer.'

Again the guns disturbed the hour,
Roaring their readiness to avenge,
As far inland as Stourton Tower,
And Camelot, and starlit Stonehenge.

April 1914

248 *The Convergence of the Twain*

(Lines on the loss of the 'Titanic')

I

In a solitude of the sea
Deep from human vanity,
And the Pride of Life that planned her, stilly couches she.

II

Steel chambers, late the pyres
Of her salamandrine fires,
Cold currents thrid, and turn to rhythmic tidal lyres.

III

Over the mirrors meant
To glass the opulent
The sea-worm crawls – grotesque, slimed, dumb, indifferent.

IV

Jewels in joy designed
To ravish the sensuous mind
Lie lightless, all their sparkles bleared and black and blind.

V

Dim moon-eyed fishes near
Gaze at the gilded gear
And query: 'What does this vaingloriousness down here?' ...

VI

Well: while was fashioning
This creature of cleaving wing,
The Immanent Will that stirs and urges everything

VII

Prepared a sinister mate
For her – so gaily great –
A Shape of Ice, for the time far and dissociate.

VIII

And as the smart ship grew
In stature, grace, and hue,
In shadowy silent distance grew the Iceberg too.

IX

Alien they seemed to be:
No mortal eye could see
The intimate welding of their later history,

X

Or sign that they were bent
By paths coincident
On being anon twin halves of one august event,

XI

Till the Spinner of the Years
Said 'Now!' And each one hears,
And consummation comes, and jars two hemispheres.

250 After the Visit

(*To F.E.D.*)

COME again to the place
Where your presence was as a leaf that skims
Down a drouthy way whose ascent bedims
  The bloom on the farer's face.

Come again, with the feet
That were light on the green as a thistledown ball,
And those mute ministrations to one and to all
  Beyond a man's saying sweet.

Until then the faint scent
Of the bordering flowers swam unheeded away,
And I marked not the charm in the changes of day
  As the cloud-colours came and went.

Through the dark corridors
Your walk was so soundless I did not know
Your form from a phantom's of long ago
  Said to pass on the ancient floors,

Till you drew from the shade,
And I saw the large luminous living eyes
Regard me in fixed inquiring-wise
  As those of a soul that weighed,

Scarce consciously,
The eternal question of what Life was,
And why we were there, and by whose strange laws
  That which mattered most could not be.

(1870)

WHEN I set out for Lyonnesse,
A hundred miles away,
The rime was on the spray,
And starlight lit my lonesomeness
When I set out for Lyonnesse
A hundred miles away.

What would bechance at Lyonnesse
While I should sojourn there
No prophet durst declare,
Nor did the wisest wizard guess
What would bechance at Lyonnesse
While I should sojourn there.

When I came back from Lyonnesse
With magic in my eyes,
All marked with mute surmise
My radiance rare and fathomless,
When I came back from Lyonnesse
With magic in my eyes!

257 Beyond the Last Lamp

(Near Tooting Common)

I

WHILE rain, with eve in partnership,
Descended darkly, drip, drip, drip,
Beyond the last lone lamp I passed
    Walking slowly, whispering sadly,
     Two linked loiterers, wan, downcast:
Some heavy thought constrained each face,
And blinded them to time and place.

II

The pair seemed lovers, yet absorbed
In mental scenes no longer orbed
By love's young rays. Each countenance
    As it slowly, as it sadly
     Caught the lamplight's yellow glance,
Held in suspense a misery
At things which had been or might be.

III

When I retrod that watery way
Some hours beyond the droop of day,
Still I found pacing there the twain
    Just as slowly, just as sadly,
     Heedless of the night and rain.
One could but wonder who they were
And what wild woe detained them there.

IV

Though thirty years of blur and blot
Have slid since I beheld that spot,
And saw in curious converse there
    Moving slowly, moving sadly
     That mysterious tragic pair,
Its olden look may linger on –
All but the couple; they have gone.

Whither? Who knows, indeed. . . . And yet
To me, when nights are weird and wet,
Without those comrades there at tryst
    Creeping slowly, creeping sadly,
      That lone lane does not exist.
There they seem brooding on their pain,
And will, while such a lane remain.

259 *Lost Love*

I PLAY my sweet old airs –
    The airs he knew
    When our love was true –
    But he does not balk
    His determined walk,
And passes up the stairs.

I sing my songs once more,
    And presently hear
    His footstep near
    As if it would stay;
    But he goes his way,
And shuts a distant door.

So I wait for another morn,
    And another night
    In this soul-sick blight;
    And I wonder much
    As I sit, why such
A woman as I was born!

MY spirit will not haunt the mound
    Above my breast,
But travel, memory-possessed,
To where my tremulous being found
    Life largest, best.

My phantom-footed shape will go
    When nightfall grays
Hither and thither along the ways
I and another used to know
    In backward days.

And there you'll find me, if a jot
    You still should care
For me, and for my curious air;
If otherwise, then I shall not,
    For you, be there.

261 Wessex Heights

(1896)

THERE are some heights in Wessex, shaped as if by a kindly hand
For thinking, dreaming, dying on, and at crises when I stand,
Say, on Ingpen Beacon eastward, or on Wylls-Neck westwardly,
I seem where I was before my birth, and after death may be.

In the lowlands I have no comrade, not even the lone man's friend –
Her who suffereth long and is kind; accepts what he is too weak to
    mend:
Down there they are dubious and askance; there nobody thinks as I,
But mind-chains do not clank where one's next neighbour is the sky.

In the towns I am tracked by phantoms having weird detective ways –
Shadows of beings who fellowed with myself of earlier days:
They hang about at places, and they say harsh heavy things –
Men with a wintry sneer, and women with tart disparagings.

Down there I seem to be false to myself, my simple self that was,
And is not now, and I see him watching, wondering what crass cause
Can have merged him into such a strange continuator as this,
Who yet has something in common with himself, my chrysalis.

I cannot go to the great grey Plain; there's a figure against the moon,
Nobody sees it but I, and it makes my breast beat out of tune;
I cannot go to the tall-spired town, being barred by the forms now
    passed
For everybody but me, in whose long vision they stand there fast.

There's a ghost at Yell'ham Bottom chiding loud at the fall of the
    night,
There's a ghost in Froom-side Vale, thin-lipped and vague, in a shroud
    of white,
There is one in the railway train whenever I do not want it near,
I see its profile against the pane, saying what I would not hear.

As for one rare fair woman, I am now but a thought of hers,
I enter her mind and another thought succeeds me that she prefers;
Yet my love for her in its fulness she herself even did not know;
Well, time cures hearts of tenderness, and now I can let her go.

So I am found on Ingpen Beacon, or on Wylls-Neck to the west,
Or else on homely Bulbarrow, or little Pilsdon Crest,
Where men have never cared to haunt, nor women have walked with
    me,
And ghosts then keep their distance; and I know some liberty.

WHEN you slowly emerged from the den of Time,
And gained percipience as you grew,
And fleshed you fair out of shapeless slime,

Wherefore, O Man, did there come to you
The unhappy need of creating me –
A form like your own – for praying to?

My virtue, power, utility,
Within my maker must all abide,
Since none in myself can ever be,

One thin as a phasm on a lantern-slide
Shown forth in the dark upon some dim sheet,
And by none but its showman vivified.

'Such a forced device,' you may say, 'is meet
For easing a loaded heart at whiles:
Man needs to conceive of a mercy-seat

Somewhere above the gloomy aisles
Of this wailful world, or he could not bear
The irk no local hope beguiles.'

– But since I was framed in your first despair
The doing without me has had no play
In the minds of men when shadows scare;

And now that I dwindle day by day
Beneath the deicide eyes of seers
In a light that will not let me stay,

And to-morrow the whole of me disappears,
The truth should be told, and the fact be faced
That had best been faced in earlier years:

The fact of life with dependence placed
On the human heart's resource alone,
In brotherhood bonded close and graced

With loving-kindness fully blown,
And visioned help unsought, unknown.

1909–10

I

I SAW a slowly-stepping train –
Lined on the brows, scoop-eyed and bent and hoar –
Following in files across a twilit plain
A strange and mystic form the foremost bore.

II

And by contagious throbs of thought
Or latent knowledge that within me lay
And had already stirred me, I was wrought
To consciousness of sorrow even as they.

III

The fore-borne shape, to my blurred eyes,
At first seemed man-like, and anon to change
To an amorphous cloud of marvellous size,
At times endowed with wings of glorious range.

IV

And this phantasmal variousness
Ever possessed it as they drew along:
Yet throughout all it symboled none the less
Potency vast and loving-kindness strong.

V

Almost before I knew I bent
Towards the moving columns without a word;
They, growing in bulk and numbers as they went,
Struck out sick thoughts that could be overheard: –

VI

'O man-projected Figure, of late
Imaged as we, thy knell who shall survive?
Whence came it we were tempted to create
One whom we can no longer keep alive?

VII

'Framing him jealous, fierce, at first,
We gave him justice as the ages rolled,
Will to bless those by circumstance accurst,
And longsuffering, and mercies manifold.

VIII

'And, tricked by our own early dream
And need of solace, we grew self-deceived,
Our making soon our maker did we deem,
And what we had imagined we believed.

IX

'Till, in Time's stayless stealthy swing,
Uncompromising rude reality
Mangled the Monarch of our fashioning,
Who quavered, sank; and now has ceased to be.

X

'So, toward our myth's oblivion,
Darkling, and languid-lipped, we creep and grope
Sadlier than those who wept in Babylon,
Whose Zion was a still abiding hope.

XI

'How sweet it was in years far hied
To start the wheels of day with trustful prayer,
To lie down liegely at the eventide
And feel a blest assurance he was there!

XII

'And who or what shall fill his place?
Whither will wanderers turn distracted eyes
For some fixed star to stimulate their pace
Towards the goal of their enterprise?' . . .

XIII

Some in the background then I saw,
Sweet women, youths, men, all incredulous,
Who chimed: 'This is a counterfeit of straw,
This requiem mockery! Still he lives to us!'

XIV

I could not buoy their faith: and yet
Many I had known: with all I sympathized;
And though struck speechless, I did not forget
That what was mourned for, I, too, long had prized.

XV

Still, how to bear such loss I deemed
The insistent question for each animate mind,
And gazing, to my growing sight there seemed
A pale yet positive gleam low down behind,

XVI

Whereof, to lift the general night,
A certain few who stood aloof had said,
'See you upon the horizon that small light –
Swelling somewhat?' Each mourner shook his head.

XVII

And they composed a crowd of whom
Some were right good, and many nigh the best. . . .
Thus dazed and puzzled 'twixt the gleam and gloom
Mechanically I followed with the rest.

1908–10

I

LOOKING forward to the spring
One puts up with anything.
On this February day
Though the winds leap down the street
Wintry scourgings seem but play,
And these later shafts of sleet
– Sharper pointed than the first –
And these later snows – the worst –
Are as a half-transparent blind
Riddled by rays from sun behind.

II

Shadows of the October pine
Reach into this room of mine:
On the pine there swings a bird;
He is shadowed with the tree.
Mutely perched he bills no word;
Blank as I am even is he.
For those happy suns are past,
Fore-discerned in winter last.
When went by their pleasure, then?
I, alas, perceived not when.

274 At Day-Close in November

THE ten hours' light is abating,
    And a late bird wings across,
Where the pines, like waltzers waiting,
    Give their black heads a toss.

Beech leaves, that yellow the noon-time,
    Float past like specks in the eye;
I set every tree in my June time,
    And now they obscure the sky.

And the children who ramble through here
    Conceive that there never has been
A time when no tall trees grew here,
    That none will in time be seen.

276 Under the Waterfall

'WHENEVER I plunge my arm, like this,
In a basin of water, I never miss
The sweet sharp sense of a fugitive day
Fetched back from its thickening shroud of gray.
    Hence the only prime
    And real love-rhyme
    That I know by heart,
    And that leaves no smart,
Is the purl of a little valley fall
About three spans wide and two spans tall
Over a table of solid rock,
And into a scoop of the self-same block;
The purl of a runlet that never ceases
In stir of kingdoms, in wars, in peaces;
With a hollow boiling voice it speaks
And has spoken since hills were turfless peaks.'

'And why gives this the only prime
Idea to you of a real love-rhyme?
And why does plunging your arm in a bowl
Full of spring water, bring throbs to your soul?'

'Well, under the fall, in a crease of the stone,
Though where precisely none ever has known,
Jammed darkly, nothing to show how prized,
And by now with its smoothness opalized,
      Is a drinking-glass:
      For, down that pass
      My lover and I
      Walked under a sky
Of blue with a leaf-wove awning of green,
In the burn of August, to paint the scene,
And we placed our basket of fruit and wine
By the runlet's rim, where we sat to dine;
And when we had drunk from the glass together,
Arched by the oak-copse from the weather,
I held the vessel to rinse in the fall,
Where it slipped, and sank, and was past recall,
Though we stooped and plumbed the little abyss
With long bared arms. There the glass still is.
And, as said, if I thrust my arm below
Cold water in basin or bowl, a throe
From the past awakens a sense of that time,
And the glass we used, and the cascade's rhyme.
The basin seems the pool, and its edge
The hard smooth face of the brook-side ledge,
And the leafy pattern of china-ware
The hanging plants that were bathing there.

'By night, by day, when it shines or lours,
There lies intact that chalice of ours,
And its presence adds to the rhyme of love
Persistently sung by the fall above.
No lip has touched it since his and mine
In turns therefrom sipped lovers' wine.'

POEMS OF 1912–13

This sequence of poems, printed here in its entirety and numbered 277–297, arose out of Hardy's emotions at the death of his first wife Emma Lavinia in 1912. During her lifetime he had found it difficult to express, or even to feel, love for her, but after her death he made a journey to Cornwall, revisiting the scenes of their first happiness, and these poems resulted.

277 The Going

WHY did you give no hint that night
That quickly after the morrow's dawn,
And calmly, as if indifferent quite,
You would close your term here, up and be gone
    Where I could not follow
    With wing of swallow
To gain one glimpse of you ever anon!

    Never to bid good-bye,
    Or lip me the softest call,
Or utter a wish for a word, while I
Saw morning harden upon the wall,
    Unmoved, unknowing
    That your great going
Had place that moment, and altered all.

Why do you make me leave the house
And think for a breath it is you I see
At the end of the alley of bending boughs
Where so often at dusk you used to be;
    Till in darkening dankness
    The yawning blankness
Of the perspective sickens me!

    You were she who abode
    By those red-veined rocks far West,
You were the swan-necked one who rode
Along the beetling Beeny Crest,
    And, reining nigh me,
    Would muse and eye me,
While Life unrolled us its very best.

Why, then, latterly did we not speak,
Did we not think of those days long dead,

And ere your vanishing strive to seek
That time's renewal? We might have said,
    'In this bright spring weather
    We'll visit together
Those places that once we visited.'

    Well, well! All's past amend,
    Unchangeable. It must go.
I seem but a dead man held on end
To sink down soon. . . . O you could not know
    That such swift fleeing
    No soul foreseeing –
Not even I – would undo me so!

December 1912

278 *Your Last Drive*

HERE by the moorway you returned,
And saw the borough lights ahead
That lit your face – all undiscerned
To be in a week the face of the dead,
And you told of the charm of that haloed view
That never again would beam on you.

And on your left you passed the spot
Where eight days later you were to lie,
And be spoken of as one who was not;
Beholding it with a heedless eye
As alien from you, though under its tree
You soon would halt everlastingly.

I drove not with you. . . . Yet had I sat
At your side that eve I should not have seen
That the countenance I was glancing at
Had a last-time look in the flickering sheen,
Nor have read the writing upon your face,
'I go hence soon to my resting-place;

'You may miss me then. But I shall not know
How many times you visit me there,
Or what your thoughts are, or if you go
There never at all. And I shall not care.
Should you censure me I shall take no heed,
And even your praises no more shall need.'

True: never you'll know. And you will not mind.
But shall I then slight you because of such?
Dear ghost, in the past did you ever find
The thought 'What profit,' move me much?
Yet abides the fact, indeed, the same, –
You are past love, praise, indifference, blame.

December 1912

279 *The Walk*

You did not walk with me
Of late to the hill-top tree
    By the gated ways,
    As in earlier days;
    You were weak and lame,
    So you never came,
And I went alone, and I did not mind,
Not thinking of you as left behind.

I walked up there to-day
Just in the former way;
    Surveyed around
    The familiar ground
    By myself again:
    What difference, then?
Only that underlying sense
Of the look of a room on returning thence.

280 Rain on a Grave

CLOUDS spout upon her
 Their waters amain
 In ruthless disdain, –
Her who but lately
 Had shivered with pain
As at touch of dishonour
If there had lit on her
So coldly, so straightly
 Such arrows of rain:

One who to shelter
 Her delicate head
Would quicken and quicken
 Each tentative tread
If drops chanced to pelt her
 That summertime spills
 In dust-paven rills
When thunder-clouds thicken
 And birds close their bills.

Would that I lay there
 And she were housed here!
Or better, together
 Were folded away there
Exposed to one weather
We both, – who would stray there
When sunny the day there,
 Or evening was clear
 At the prime of the year.

Soon will be growing
 Green blades from her mound,
And daisies be showing
 Like stars on the ground,
Till she form part of them –
Ay – the sweet heart of them,
Loved beyond measure
With a child's pleasure
 All her life's round.

31 Jan. 1913

I FOUND her out there
On a slope few see,
That falls westwardly
To the salt-edged air,
Where the ocean breaks
On the purple strand,
And the hurricane shakes
The solid land.

I brought her here,
And have laid her to rest
In a noiseless nest
No sea beats near.
She will never be stirred
In her loamy cell
By the waves long heard
And loved so well.

So she does not sleep
By those haunted heights
The Atlantic smites
And the blind gales sweep,
Whence she often would gaze
At Dundagel's famed head,
While the dipping blaze
Dyed her face fire-red;

And would sigh at the tale
Of sunk Lyonnesse,
As a wind-tugged tress
Flapped her cheek like a flail;

Or listen at whiles
With a thought-bound brow
To the murmuring miles
She is far from now.

Yet her shade, maybe,
Will creep underground
Till it catch the sound

Of that western sea
As it swells and sobs
Where she once domiciled,
And joy in its throbs
With the heart of a child.

282 *Without Ceremony*

It was your way, my dear,
To vanish without a word
When callers, friends, or kin
Had left, and I hastened in
To rejoin you, as I inferred.

And when you'd a mind to career
Off anywhere – say to town –
You were all on a sudden gone
Before I had thought thereon,
Or noticed your trunks were down.

So, now that you disappear
For ever in that swift style,
Your meaning seems to me
Just as it used to be:
'Good-bye is not worth while!'

How she would have loved
A party to-day! –
Bright-hatted and gloved,
With table and tray
And chairs on the lawn
Her smiles would have shone
With welcomings. . . . But
She is shut, she is shut
    From friendship's spell
    In the jailing shell
    Of her tiny cell.

Or she would have reigned
At a dinner to-night
With ardours unfeigned,
And a generous delight;
All in her abode
She'd have freely bestowed
On her guests. . . . But alas,
She is shut under grass
    Where no cups flow,
    Powerless to know
    That it might be so.

And she would have sought
With a child's eager glance
The shy snowdrops brought
By the new year's advance,
And peered in the rime
Of Candlemas-time
For crocuses . . . chanced
It that she were not tranced
    From sights she loved best;
    Wholly possessed
    By an infinite rest!

And we are here staying
Amid these stale things,

Who care not for gaying,
And those junketings
That used so to joy her,
And never to cloy her
As us they cloy! . . . But
She is shut, she is shut
    From the cheer of them, dead
    To all done and said
    In her yew-arched bed.

284 *The Haunter*

HE does not think that I haunt here nightly:
    How shall I let him know
That whither his fancy sets him wandering
    I, too, alertly go? –
Hover and hover a few feet from him
    Just as I used to do,
But cannot answer the words he lifts me –
    Only listen thereto!

When I could answer he did not say them:
    When I could let him know
How I would like to join in his journeys
    Seldom he wished to go.
Now that he goes and wants me with him
    More than he used to do,
Never he sees my faithful phantom
    Though he speaks thereto.

Yes, I companion him to places
    Only dreamers know,
Where the shy hares print long paces,
    Where the night rooks go;

Into old aisles where the past is all to him,
    Close as his shade can do,
Always lacking the power to call him,
    Near as I reach thereto!

What a good haunter I am, O tell him!
    Quickly make him know
If he but sigh since my loss befell him
    Straight to his side I go.
Tell him a faithful one is doing
    All that love can do
Still that his path may be worth pursuing,
    And to bring peace thereto.

285 *The Voice*

WOMAN much missed, how you call to me, call to me,
Saying that now you are not as you were
When you had changed from the one who was all to me,
But as at first, when our day was fair.

Can it be you that I hear? Let me view you, then,
Standing as when I drew near to the town
Where you would wait for me: yes, as I knew you then,
Even to the original air-blue gown!

Or is it only the breeze, in its listlessness
Travelling across the wet mead to me here,
You being ever dissolved to wan wistlessness,
Heard no more again far or near?

    Thus I; faltering forward,
    Leaves around me falling,
Wind oozing thin through the thorn from norward,
    And the woman calling.

December 1912

I COME across from Mellstock while the moon wastes weaker
To behold where I lived with you for twenty years and more:
I shall go in the gray, at the passing of the mail-train,
And need no setting open of the long familiar door
        As before.

The change I notice in my once own quarters!
A formal-fashioned border where the daisies used to be,
The rooms new painted, and the pictures altered,
And other cups and saucers, and no cosy nook for tea
        As with me.

I discern the dim faces of the sleep-wrapt servants;
They are not those who tended me through feeble hours and strong,
But strangers quite, who never knew my rule here,
Who never saw me painting, never heard my softling song
        Float along.

So I don't want to linger in this re-decked dwelling,
I feel too uneasy at the contrasts I behold,
And I make again for Mellstock to return here never,
And rejoin the roomy silence, and the mute and manifold
        Souls of old.

1913

287 A Circular

As 'legal representative'
I read a missive not my own,
On new designs the senders give
    For clothes, in tints as shown.

Here figure blouses, gowns for tea,
And presentation-trains of state,
Charming ball-dresses, millinery,
    Warranted up to date.

And this gay-pictured, spring-time shout
Of Fashion, hails what lady proud?
Her who before last year ebbed out
    Was costumed in a shroud.

288 A Dream or No

WHY go to Saint-Juliot? What's Juliot to me?
    Some strange necromancy
    But charmed me to fancy
That much of my life claims the spot as its key.

Yes. I have had dreams of that place in the West,
    And a maiden abiding
    Thereat as in hiding;
Fair-eyed and white-shouldered, broad-browed and brown-tressed.

And of how, coastward bound on a night long ago,
    There lonely I found her,
    The sea-birds around her,
And other than nigh things uncaring to know.

So sweet her life there (in my thought has it seemed)
    That quickly she drew me
    To take her unto me,
And lodge her long years with me. Such have I dreamed.

But nought of that maid from Saint-Juliot I see;
     Can she ever have been here,
     And shed her life's sheen here,
The woman I thought a long housemate with me?

Does there even a place like Saint-Juliot exist?
     Or a Vallency Valley
     With stream and leafed alley,
Or Beeny, or Bos with its flounce flinging mist?

February 1913

289 *After a Journey*

HERETO I come to view a voiceless ghost;
     Whither, O whither will its whim now draw me?
Up the cliff, down, till I'm lonely, lost,
     And the unseen waters' ejaculations awe me.
Where you will next be there's no knowing,
     Facing round about me everywhere,
          With your nut-coloured hair,
And gray eyes, and rose-flush coming and going.

Yes: I have re-entered your olden haunts at last;
     Through the years, through the dead scenes I have tracked you;
What have you now found to say of our past —
     Scanned across the dark space wherein I have lacked you?
Summer gave us sweets, but autumn wrought division?
     Things were not lastly as firstly well
          With us twain, you tell?
But all's closed now, despite Time's derision.

I see what you are doing: you are leading me on
     To the spots we knew when we haunted here together,
The waterfall, above which the mist-bow shone
     At the then fair hour in the then fair weather,
And the cave just under, with a voice still so hollow
     That it seems to call out to me from forty years ago,
          When you were all aglow,
And not the thin ghost that I now frailly follow!

Ignorant of what there is flitting here to see,
　　The waked birds preen and the seals flop lazily;
Soon you will have, Dear, to vanish from me,
　　For the stars close their shutters and the dawn whitens hazily.
Trust me, I mind not, though Life lours,
　　The bringing me here; nay, bring me here again!
　　　　I am just the same as when
Our days were a joy, and our paths through flowers.

Pentargan Bay

290 *A Death-Day Recalled*

BEENY did not quiver,
　　Juliot grew not gray,
Thin Vallency's river
　　Held its wonted way.
Bos seemed not to utter
　　Dimmest note of dirge,
Targan mouth a mutter
　　To its creamy surge.

Yet though these, unheeding,
　　Listless, passed the hour
Of her spirit's speeding,
　　She had, in her flower,
Sought and loved the places –
　　Much and often pined
For their lonely faces
　　When in towns confined.

Why did not Vallency
　　In his purl deplore
One whose haunts were whence he
　　Drew his limpid store?
Why did Bos not thunder,
　　Targan apprehend
Body and Breath were sunder
　　Of their former friend?

291 Beeny Cliff

March 1870–March 1913

I

O THE opal and the sapphire of that wandering western sea,
And the woman riding high above with bright hair flapping free –
The woman whom I loved so, and who loyally loved me.

II

The pale mews plained below us, and the waves seemed far away
In a nether sky, engrossed in saying their ceaseless babbling say,
As we laughed light-heartedly aloft on that clear-sunned March day.

III

A little cloud then cloaked us, and there flew an irised rain,
And the Atlantic dyed its levels with a dull misfeatured stain,
And then the sun burst out again, and purples prinked the main.

IV

– Still in all its chasmal beauty bulks old Beeny to the sky,
And shall she and I not go there once again now March is nigh,
And the sweet things said in that March say anew there by and by?

V

What if still in chasmal beauty looms that wild weird western shore,
The woman now is – elsewhere – whom the ambling pony bore,
And nor knows nor cares for Beeny, and will laugh there nevermore.

As I drive to the junction of lane and highway,
   And the drizzle bedrenches the waggonette,
I look behind at the fading byway,
   And see on its slope, now glistening wet,
     Distinctly yet

Myself and a girlish form benighted
   In dry March weather. We climb the road
Beside a chaise. We had just alighted
   To ease the sturdy pony's load
     When he sighed and slowed.

What we did as we climbed, and what we talked of
   Matters not much, nor to what it led, –
Something that life will not be balked of
   Without rude reason till hope is dead,
     And feeling fled.

It filled but a minute. But was there ever
   A time of such quality, since or before,
In that hill's story? To one mind never,
   Though it has been climbed, foot-swift, foot-sore,
     By thousands more.

Primaeval rocks form the road's steep border,
   And much have they faced there, first and last,
Of the transitory in Earth's long order;
   But what they record in colour and cast
     Is – that we two passed.

And to me, though Time's unflinching rigour,
   In mindless rote, has ruled from sight
The substance now, one phantom figure
   Remains on the slope, as when that night
     Saw us alight.

I look and see it there, shrinking, shrinking,
   I look back at it amid the rain
For the very last time; for my sand is sinking,
   And I shall traverse old love's domain
     Never again.

March 1913

NOBODY says: Ah, that is the place
Where chanced, in the hollow of years ago,
What none of the Three Towns cared to know –
The birth of a little girl of grace –
The sweetest the house saw, first or last;
      Yet it was so
      On that day long past.

Nobody thinks: There, there she lay
In a room by the Hoe, like the bud of a flower,
And listened, just after the bedtime hour,
To the stammering chimes that used to play
The quaint Old Hundred-and-Thirteenth tune
      In Saint Andrew's tower
      Night, morn, and noon.

Nobody calls to mind that here
Upon Boterel Hill, where the waggoners skid,
With cheeks whose airy flush outbid
Fresh fruit in bloom, and free of fear,
She cantered down, as if she must fall
      (Though she never did),
      To the charm of all.

Nay: one there is to whom these things,
That nobody else's mind calls back,
Have a savour that scenes in being lack,
And a presence more than the actual brings;
To whom to-day is beneaped and stale,
      And its urgent clack
      But a vapid tale.

Plymouth, March 1913

I

QUEER are the ways of a man I know:
    He comes and stands
    In a careworn craze,
    And looks at the sands
    And the seaward haze
    With moveless hands
    And face and gaze,
    Then turns to go . . .
And what does he see when he gazes so?

II

They say he sees as an instant thing
    More clear than to-day,
    A sweet soft scene
    That was once in play
    By that briny green;
    Yes, notes alway
    Warm, real, and keen,
    What his back years bring –
A phantom of his own figuring.

III

Of this vision of his they might say more:
    Not only there
    Does he see this sight,
    But everywhere
    In his brain – day, night,
    As if on the air
    It were drawn rose-bright –
    Yea, far from that shore
Does he carry this vision of heretofore:

IV

A ghost-girl-rider. And though, toil-tried,
    He withers daily,
    Time touches her not,

But she still rides gaily
In his rapt thought
On that shagged and shaly
Atlantic spot,
And as when first eyed
Draws rein and sings to the swing of the tide.

1913

295 *The Spell of the Rose*

'I MEAN to build a hall anon,
    And shape two turrets there,
    And a broad newelled stair,
And a cool well for crystal water;
    Yes; I will build a hall anon,
    Plant roses love shall feed upon,
        And apple-trees and pear.'

He set to build the manor-hall,
    And shaped the turrets there,
    And the broad newelled stair,
And the cool well for crystal water;
    He built for me that manor-hall,
    And planted many trees withal,
        But no rose anywhere.

And as he planted never a rose
    That bears the flower of love,
    Though other flowers throve
Some heart-bane moved our souls to sever
    Since he had planted never a rose;
    And misconceits raised horrid shows,
        And agonies came thereof.

'I'll mend these miseries,' then said I,
  And so, at dead of night,
  I went and, screened from sight,
That nought should keep our souls in severance,
I set a rose-bush. 'This,' said I,
  'May end divisions dire and wry,
  And long-drawn days of blight.'

But I was called from earth – yea, called
  Before my rose-bush grew;
  And would that now I knew
What feels he of the tree I planted,
  And whether, after I was called
  To be a ghost, he, as of old,
  Gave me his heart anew!

Perhaps now blooms that queen of trees
  I set but saw not grow,
  And he, beside its glow –
Eyes couched of the mis-vision that blurred me –
  Ay, there beside that queen of trees
  He sees me as I was, though sees
  Too late to tell me so!

SLIP back, Time!
Yet again I am nearing
Castle and keep, uprearing
  Gray, as in my prime.

  At the inn
Smiling nigh, why is it
Not as on my visit
  When hope and I were twin?

  Groom and jade
Whom I found here, moulder;
Strange the tavern-holder,
  Strange the tap-maid.

  Here I hired
Horse and man for bearing
Me on my wayfaring
  To the door desired.

  Evening gloomed
As I journeyed forward
To the faces shoreward,
  Till their dwelling loomed.

  If again
Towards the Atlantic sea there
I should speed, they'd be there
  Surely now as then? . . .

  Why waste thought,
When I know them vanished
Under earth; yea, banished
  Ever into nought!

WHERE we made the fire
In the summer time
Of branch and briar
On the hill to the sea,
I slowly climb
Through winter mire,
And scan and trace
The forsaken place
Quite readily.

Now a cold wind blows,
And the grass is gray,
But the spot still shows
As a burnt circle – aye,
And stick-ends, charred,
Still strew the sward
Whereon I stand,
Last relic of the band
Who came that day!

Yes, I am here
Just as last year,
And the sea breathes brine
From its strange straight line
Up hither, the same
As when we four came.

– But two have wandered far
From this grassy rise
Into urban roar
Where no picnics are,
And one – has shut her eyes
For evermore

'Where the Picnic Was' completes the sequence of
Poems of 1912–13

303 She Charged Me

SHE charged me with having said this and that
To another woman long years before,
In the very parlour where we sat, –

Sat on a night when the endless pour
Of rain on the roof and the road below
Bent the spring of the spirit more and more. . . .

– So charged she me; and the Cupid's bow
Of her mouth was hard, and her eyes, and her face,
And her white forefinger lifted slow.

Had she done it gently, or shown a trace
That not too curiously would she view
A folly flown ere her reign had place,

A kiss might have closed it. But I knew
From the fall of each word, and the pause between,
That the curtain would drop upon us two
Ere long, in our play of slave and queen.

THE chimes called midnight, just at interlune,
And the daytime parle on the Roman investigations
Was shut to silence, save for the husky tune
The bubbling waters played near the excavations.

And a warm air came up from underground,
And the flutter of a filmy shape unsepulchred,
That collected itself, and waited, and looked around:
Nothing was seen, but utterances could be heard:

Those of the Goddess whose shrine was beneath the pile
Of the God with the baldachined altar overhead:
'And what did you win by raising this nave and aisle
Close on the site of the temple I tenanted?

'The notes of your organ have thrilled down out of view
To the earth-clogged wrecks of my edifice many a year,
Though stately and shining once – ay, long ere you
Had set up crucifix and candle here.

'Your priests have trampled the dust of mine without rueing,
Despising the joys of man whom I so much loved,
Though my springs boil on by your Gothic arcades and pewing,
And sculptures crude. . . . Would Jove they could be removed!'

'Repress, O lady proud, your traditional ires;
You know not by what a frail thread we equally hang;
It is said we are images both – twitched by people's desires;
And that I, as you, fail like a song men yesterday sang!'

'What – a Jumping-jack you, and myself but a poor Jumping-jill,
Now worm-eaten, times agone twitched at Humanity's bid?
O I cannot endure it! – But, chance to us whatso there will,
Let us kiss and be friends! Come, agree you?' – None heard if he did. . . .

And the olden dark hid the cavities late laid bare,
And all was suspended and soundless as before,
Except for a gossamery noise fading off in the air,
And the boiling voice of the waters' medicinal pour.

Bath

'MAN, you too, aren't you, one of these rough followers of the
      criminal?
All hanging hereabout to gather how he's going to bear
Examination in the hall.' She flung disdainful glances on
The shabby figure standing at the fire with others there,
      Who warmed them by its flare.

'No indeed, my skipping maiden: I know nothing of the trial here,
Or criminal, if so he be. – I chanced to come this way,
And the fire shone out into the dawn, and morning airs are cold now;
I, too, was drawn in part by charms I see before me play,
      That I see not every day.'

'Ha, ha!' then laughed the constables who also stood to warm them-
      selves,
The while another maiden scrutinized his features hard,
As the blaze threw into contrast every line and knot that wrinkled
      them,
Exclaiming, 'Why, last night when he was brought in by the guard,
      You were with him in the yard!'

'Nay, nay, you teasing wench, I say! You know you speak mistakenly.
Cannot a tired pedestrian who has legged it long and far
Here on his way from northern parts, engrossed in humble marketings,
Come in and rest awhile, although judicial doings are
      Afoot by morning star?'

'O, come, come!' laughed the constables. 'Why, man, you speak the
      dialect
He uses in his answers; you can hear him up the stairs.
So own it. We sha'n't hurt ye. There he's speaking now! His syllables
Are those you sound yourself when you are talking unawares,
      As this pretty girl declares.'

'And you shudder when his chain clinks!' she rejoined. 'O yes, I
      noticed it.
And you winced, too, when those cuffs they gave him echoed to us
      here.
They'll soon be coming down, and you may then have to defend
      yourself

Unless you hold your tongue, or go away and keep you clear
  When he's led to judgment near!'

'No! I'll be damned in hell if I know anything about the man!
No single thing about him more than everybody knows!
Must not I even warm my hands but I am charged with blas-
  phemies?' . . .
– His face convulses as the morning cock that moment crows,
  And he droops, and turns, and goes.

318 Regret Not Me

REGRET not me;
  Beneath the sunny tree
I lie uncaring, slumbering peacefully.

Swift as the light
  I flew my faery flight;
Ecstatically I moved, and feared no night.

I did not know
  That heydays fade and go,
But deemed that what was would be always so.

I skipped at morn
  Between the yellowing corn,
Thinking it good and glorious to be born.

I ran at eves
  Among the piled-up sheaves,
Dreaming, 'I grieve not, therefore nothing grieves.'

Now soon will come
  The apple, pear, and plum,
And hinds will sing, and autumn insects hum.

Again you will fare
  To cider-makings rare,
And junketings; but I shall not be there.

Yet gaily sing
Until the pewter ring
Those songs we sang when we went gipsying.

And lightly dance
Some triple-timed romance
In coupled figures, and forget mischance;

And mourn not me
Beneath the yellowing tree;
For I shall mind not, slumbering peacefully.

325 *Seen by the Waits*

THROUGH snowy woods and shady
    We went to play a tune
To the lonely manor-lady
    By the light of the Christmas moon.

We violed till, upward glancing
    To where a mirror leaned,
It showed her airily dancing,
    Deeming her movements screened;

Dancing alone in the room there,
    Thin-draped in her robe of night;
Her postures, glassed in the gloom there,
    Were a strange phantasmal sight.

She had learnt (we heard when homing)
    That her roving spouse was dead:
Why she had danced in the gloaming
    We thought, but never said.

'SEE, here's the workbox, little wife,
   That I made of polished oak.'
He was a joiner, of village life;
   She came of borough folk.

He holds the present up to her
   As with a smile she nears
And answers to the profferer,
   ''Twill last all my sewing years!'

'I warrant it will. And longer too.
   'Tis a scantling that I got
Off poor John Wayward's coffin, who
   Died of they knew not what.

'The shingled pattern that seems to cease
   Against your box's rim
Continues right on in the piece
   That's underground with him.

'And while I worked it made me think
   Of timber's varied doom;
One inch where people eat and drink,
   The next inch in a tomb.

'But why do you look so white, my dear,
   And turn aside your face?
You knew not that good lad, I fear,
   Though he came from your native place?'

'How could I know that good young man,
   Though he came from my native town,
When he must have left far earlier than
   I was a woman grown?'

'Ah, no. I should have understood!
   It shocked you that I gave
To you one end of a piece of wood
   Whose other is in a grave?'

'Don't, dear, despise my intellect,
    Mere accidental things
Of that sort never have effect
    On my imaginings.'

Yet still her lips were limp and wan,
    Her face still held aside,
As if she had known not only John,
    But known of what he died.

From 'Satires of Circumstance,
in Fifteen Glimpses'

337 I. At Tea

THE kettle descants in a cosy drone,
And the young wife looks in her husband's face,
And then at her guest's, and shows in her own
Her sense that she fills an envied place;
And the visiting lady is all abloom,
And says there was never so sweet a room.

And the happy young housewife does not know
That the woman beside her was first his choice,
Till the fates ordained it could not be so. . . .
Betraying nothing in look or voice
The guest sits smiling and sips her tea,
And he throws her a stray glance yearningly.

338 II. In Church

'AND now to God the Father,' he ends,
And his voice thrills up to the topmost tiles:
Each listener chokes as he bows and bends,
And emotion pervades the crowded aisles.
Then the preacher glides to the vestry-door,
And shuts it, and thinks he is seen no more.

The door swings softly ajar meanwhile,
And a pupil of his in the Bible class,
Who adores him as one without gloss or guile,
Sees her idol stand with a satisfied smile
And re-enact at the vestry-glass
Each pulpit gesture in deft dumb-show
That had moved the congregation so.

342 VI. In the Cemetery

'YOU see those mothers squabbling there?'
Remarks the man of the cemetery.
'One says in tears, "'Tis mine lies here!"
Another, "Nay, mine, you Pharisee!"
Another, "How dare you move my flowers
And put your own on this grave of ours!"
But all their children were laid therein
At different times, like sprats in a tin.

'And then the main drain had to cross,
And we moved the lot some nights ago,
And packed them away in the general foss
With hundreds more. But their folks don't know,
And as well cry over a new-laid drain
As anything else, to ease your pain!'

HE enters, and mute on the edge of a chair
Sits a thin-faced lady, a stranger there,
A type of decayed gentility;
And by some small signs he well can guess
That she comes to him almost breakfastless.

'I have called – I hope I do not err –
I am looking for a purchaser
Of some score volumes of the works
Of eminent divines I own, –
Left by my father – though it irks
My patience to offer them.' And she smiles
As if necessity were unknown;
'But the truth of it is that oftenwhiles
I have wished, as I am fond of art,
To make my rooms a little smart,
And these old books are so in the way.'
And lightly still she laughs to him,
As if to sell were a mere gay whim,
And that, to be frank, Life were indeed
To her not vinegar and gall,
But fresh and honey-like; and Need
No household skeleton at all.

348 XII. At the Draper's

'I STOOD at the back of the shop, my dear,
    But you did not perceive me.
Well, when they deliver what you were shown
    I shall know nothing of it, believe me!'

And he coughed and coughed as she paled and said,
    'O, I didn't see you come in there –
Why couldn't you speak?' – 'Well, I didn't. I left
    That you should not notice I'd been there.

'You were viewing some lovely things. *"Soon required*
    For a widow, of latest fashion;"
And I knew 'twould upset you to meet the man
    Who had to be cold and ashen

'And screwed in a box before they could dress you
    "In the last new note in mourning,"
As they defined it. So, not to distress you,
    I left you to your adorning.'

354 Why Be at Pains?

(*Wooer's Song*)

WHY be at pains that I should know
    You sought not me?
Do breezes, then, make features glow
    So rosily?
Come, the lit port is at our back,
    And the tumbling sea;
Elsewhere the lampless uphill track
    To uncertainty!

O should not we two waifs join hands?
    I am alone,
You would enrich me more than lands
    By being my own.

Yet, though this facile moment flies,
    Close is your tone,
And ere to-morrow's dewfall dries
    I plough the unknown.

355 *We Sat at the Window*

(*Bournemouth, 1875*)

WE sat at the window looking out,
And the rain came down like silken strings
That Swithin's day. Each gutter and spout
Babbled unchecked in the busy way
    Of witless things:
Nothing to read, nothing to see
Seemed in that room for her and me
    On Swithin's day.

We were irked by the scene, by our own selves; yes,
For I did not know, nor did she infer
How much there was to read and guess
By her in me, and to see and crown
    By me in her.
Wasted were two souls in their prime,
And great was the waste, that July time
    When the rain came down.

356 Afternoon Service at Mellstock

(Circa 1850)

On afternoons of drowsy calm
We stood in the panelled pew,
Singing one-voiced a Tate-and-Brady psalm
To the tune of 'Cambridge New'.

We watched the elms, we watched the rooks,
The clouds upon the breeze,
Between the whiles of glancing at our books,
And swaying like the trees.

So mindless were those outpourings! –
Though I am not aware
That I have gained by subtle thought on things
Since we stood psalming there.

363 Heredity

I am the family face;
Flesh perishes, I live on,
Projecting trait and trace
Through time to times anon,
And leaping from place to place
Over oblivion.

The years-heired feature that can
In curve and voice and eye
Despise the human span
Of durance – that is I;
The eternal thing in man,
That heeds no call to die.

366 Near Lanivet, 1872

THERE was a stunted handpost just on the crest,
        Only a few feet high:
She was tired, and we stopped in the twilight-time for her rest,
        At the crossways close thereby.

She leant back, being so weary, against its stem,
        And laid her arms on its own,
Each open palm stretched out to each end of them,
        Her sad face sideways thrown.

Her white-clothed form at this dim-lit cease of day
        Made her look as one crucified
In my gaze at her from the midst of the dusty way,
        And hurriedly 'Don't,' I cried.

I do not think she heard. Loosing thence she said,
        As she stepped forth ready to go,
'I am rested now. – Something strange came into my head;
        I wish I had not leant so!'

And wordless we moved onward down from the hill
        In the west cloud's murked obscure,
And looking back we could see the handpost still
        In the solitude of the moor.

'It struck her too,' I thought, for as if afraid
        She heavily breathed as we trailed;
Till she said, 'I did not think how 'twould look in the shade,
        When I leant there like one nailed.'

I, lightly: 'There's nothing in it. For *you*, anyhow!'
        – 'O I know there is not,' said she . . .
'Yet I wonder. . . . If no one is bodily crucified now,
        In spirit one may be!'

And we dragged on and on, while we seemed to see
        In the running of Time's far glass
Her crucified, as she had wondered if she might be
        Some day. – Alas, alas!

'WHAT have you looked at, Moon,
    In your time,
   Now long past your prime?'
'O, I have looked at, often looked at
    Sweet, sublime,
Sore things, shudderful, night and noon
    In my time.'

'What have you mused on, Moon,
    In your day,
   So aloof, so far away?'
'O, I have mused on, often mused on
    Growth, decay,
Nations alive, dead, mad, aswoon,
    In my day!'

'Have you much wondered, Moon,
    On your rounds,
   Self-wrapt, beyond Earth's bounds?'
'Yea, I have wondered, often wondered
    At the sounds
Reaching me of the human tune
    On my rounds.'

'What do you think of it, Moon,
    As you go?
   Is Life much, or no?'
'O, I think of it, often think of it
    As a show
God ought surely to shut up soon,
    As I go.'

370 To Shakespeare

After Three Hundred Years

BRIGHT baffling Soul, least capturable of themes,
Thou, who display'dst a life of commonplace,
Leaving no intimate word or personal trace
Of high design outside the artistry
　　Of thy penned dreams,
Still shalt remain at heart unread eternally.

Through human orbits thy discourse to-day,
Despite thy formal pilgrimage, throbs on
In harmonies that cow Oblivion,
And, like the wind, with all-uncared effect
　　Maintain a sway
Not fore-desired, in tracks unchosen and unchecked.

And yet, at thy last breath, with mindless note
The borough clocks but samely tongued the hour,
The Avon just as always glassed the tower,
Thy age was published on thy passing-bell
　　But in due rote
With other dwellers' deaths accorded a like knell.

And at the strokes some townsman (met, maybe,
And thereon queried by some squire's good dame
Driving in shopward) may have given thy name,
With, 'Yes, a worthy man and well-to-do;
　　Though, as for me,
I knew him but by just a neighbour's nod, 'tis true.

'I' faith, few knew him much here, save by word,
He having elsewhere led his busier life;
Though to be sure he left with us his wife.'
– 'Ah, one of the tradesmen's sons, I now recall. . . .
　　Witty, I've heard. . . .
We did not know him. . . . Well, good-day. Death comes
　　to all.'

So, like a strange bright bird we sometimes find
To mingle with the barn-door brood awhile,

139

Then vanish from their homely domicile –
Into man's poesy, we wot not whence,
Flew thy strange mind,
Lodged there a radiant guest, and sped for ever thence.
1916

371 *Quid Hic Agis?*

I

WHEN I weekly knew
An ancient pew,
And murmured there
The forms of prayer
And thanks and praise
In the ancient ways,
And heard read out
During August drought
That chapter from Kings
Harvest-time brings;
– How the prophet, broken
By griefs unspoken,
Went heavily away
To fast and to pray,
And, while waiting to die,
The Lord passed by,
And a whirlwind and fire
Drew nigher and nigher,
And a small voice anon
Bade him up and be gone, –
I did not apprehend
As I sat to the end
And watched for her smile
Across the sunned aisle,
That this tale of a seer
Which came once a year

Might, when sands were heaping,
Be like a sweat creeping,
Or in any degree
Bear on her or on me!

II

When later, by chance
Of circumstance,
It befel me to read
On a hot afternoon
At the lectern there
The selfsame words
As the lesson decreed,
To the gathered few
From the hamlets near –
Folk of flocks and herds
Sitting half aswoon,
Who listened thereto
As women and men
Not overmuch
Concerned at such –
So, like them then,
I did not see
What drought might be
With me, with her,
As the Kalendar
Moved on, and Time
Devoured our prime.

III

But now, at last,
When our glory has passed,
And there is no smile
From her in the aisle,
But where it once shone
A marble, men say,
With her name thereon
Is discerned to-day;
And spiritless
In the wilderness

I shrink from sight
And desire the night,
(Though, as in old wise,
I might still arise,
Go forth, and stand
And prophesy in the land),
I feel the shake
Of wind and earthquake,
And consuming fire
Nigher and nigher,
And the voice catch clear,
'What doest thou here?'

The Spectator: 1916. During the War

372 On a Midsummer Eve

I IDLY cut a parsley stalk,
And blew therein towards the moon;
I had not thought what ghosts would walk
With shivering footsteps to my tune.

I went, and knelt, and scooped my hand
As if to drink, into the brook,
And a faint figure seemed to stand
Above me, with the bygone look.

I lipped rough rhymes of chance, not choice,
I thought not what my words might be;
There came into my ear a voice
That turned a tenderer verse for me.

373 Timing Her

(Written to an old folk-tune)

LALAGE'S coming:
Where is she now, O?
Turning to bow, O,
And smile, is she,
Just at parting,
Parting, parting,
As she is starting
To come to me?

Where is she now, O,
Now, and now, O,
Shadowing a bough, O,
Of hedge or tree
As she is rushing,
Rushing, rushing,
Gossamers brushing
To come to me?

Lalage's coming;
Where is she now, O;
Climbing the brow, O,
Of hills I see?
Yes, she is nearing,
Nearing, nearing,
Weather unfearing
To come to me.

Near is she now, O,
Now, and now, O;
Milk the rich cow, O,
Forward the tea;
Shake the down bed for her,
Linen sheets spread for her,
Drape round the head for her
Coming to me.

Lalage's coming,
She's nearer now, O,
End anyhow, O,
To-day's husbandry!

Would a gilt chair were mine,
Slippers of vair were mine,
Brushes for hair were mine
Of ivory!

What will she think, O,
She who's so comely,
Viewing how homely
A sort are we!
Nothing resplendent,
No prompt attendant,
Not one dependent
Pertaining to me!

Lalage's coming;
Where is she now, O?
Fain I'd avow, O,
Full honestly
Nought here's enough for her,
All is too rough for her,
Even my love for her
Poor in degree.

She's nearer now, O,
Still nearer now, O,
She 'tis, I vow, O,
Passing the lea.
Rush down to meet her there,
Call out and greet her there,
Never a sweeter there
Crossed to me!

Lalage's come; aye,
Come is she now, O! . . .
Does Heaven allow, O,
A meeting to be?
Yes, she is here now,
Here now, here now,
Nothing to fear now,
Here's Lalage!

DOES he want you down there
In the Nether Glooms where
The hours may be a dragging load upon him,
    As he hears the axle grind
        Round and round
    Of the great world, in the blind
        Still profound
Of the night-time? He might liven at the sound
Of your string, revealing you had not forgone him.

In the gallery west the nave,
But a few yards from his grave,
Did you, tucked beneath his chin, to his bowing
    Guide the homely harmony
        Of the quire
    Who for long years strenuously –
        Son and sire –
Caught the strains that at his fingering low or higher
From your four thin threads and eff-holes came outflowing.

And, too, what merry tunes
He would bow at nights or noons
That chanced to find him bent to lute a measure,
    When he made you speak his heart
        As in dream,
    Without book or music-chart,
        On some theme
Elusive as a jack-o'-lanthorn's gleam,
And the psalm of duty shelved for trill of pleasure.

Well, you cannot, alas,
The barrier overpass
That screens him in those Mournful Meads hereunder,
    Where no fiddling can be heard
        In the glades
    Of silentness, no bird
        Thrills the shades;
Where no viol is touched for songs or serenades,
No bowing wakes a congregation's wonder.

He must do without you now,
Stir you no more anyhow
To yearning concords taught you in your glory;
While, your strings a tangled wreck,
Once smart drawn,
Ten worm-wounds in your neck,
Purflings wan
With dust-hoar, here alone I sadly con
Your present dumbness, shape your olden story.

1916

386 *The Young Churchwarden*

WHEN he lit the candles there,
And the light fell on his hand,
And it trembled as he scanned
Her and me, his vanquished air
Hinted that his dream was done,
And I saw he had begun
To understand.

When Love's viol was unstrung,
Sore I wished the hand that shook
Had been mine that shared her book
While that evening hymn was sung,
His the victor's, as he lit
Candles where he had bidden us sit
With vanquished look.

Now her dust lies listless there,
His afar from tending hand,
What avails the victory scanned?
Does he smile from upper air:
'Ah, my friend, your dream is done;
And 'tis *you* who have begun
To understand!'

388 Lines

To a Movement in Mozart's E-Flat Symphony

SHOW me again the time
When in the Junetide's prime
We flew by meads and mountains northerly! –
Yea, to such freshness, fairness, fulness, fineness, freeness,
Love lures life on.

Show me again the day
When from the sandy bay
We looked together upon the pestered sea! –
Yea, to such surging, swaying, sighing, swelling, shrinking,
Love lures life on.

Show me again the hour
When by the pinnacled tower
We eyed each other and feared futurity! –
Yea, to such bodings, broodings, beatings, blanchings, blessings,
Love lures life on.

Show me again just this:
The moment of that kiss
Away from the prancing folk, by the strawberry-tree! –
Yea, to such rashness, ratheness, rareness, ripeness, richness,
Love lures life on.

Begun November 1898

I

I BENT in the deep of night
Over a pedigree the chronicler gave
As mine; and as I bent there, half-unrobed,
The uncurtained panes of my window-square let in the watery light
Of the moon in its old age:
And green-rheumed clouds were hurrying past where mute and cold
it globed
Like a drifting dolphin's eye seen through a lapping wave.

II

So, scanning my sire-sown tree,
And the hieroglyphs of this spouse tied to that,
With offspring mapped below in lineage,
Till the tangles troubled me,
The branches seemed to twist into a seared and cynic face
Which winked and tokened towards the window like a Mage
Enchanting me to gaze again thereat.

III

It was a mirror now,
And in it a long perspective I could trace
Of my begetters, dwindling backward each past each
All with the kindred look,
Whose names had since been inked down in their place
On the recorder's book,
Generation and generation of my mien, and build, and brow.

IV

And then did I divine
That every heave and coil and move I made
Within my brain, and in my mood and speech,
Was in the glass portrayed
As long forestalled by their so making it;
The first of them, the primest fuglemen of my line,
Being fogged in far antiqueness past surmise and reason's reach.

Said I then, sunk in tone,
'I am merest mimicker and counterfeit! –
Though thinking, *I am I,*
And what I do I do myself alone.'
– The cynic twist of the page thereat unknit
Back to its normal figure, having wrought its purport wry,
The Mage's mirror left the window-square,
And the stained moon and drift retook their places there.

1916

392 *Where They Lived*

DISHEVELLED leaves creep down
Upon that bank to-day,
Some green, some yellow, and some pale brown;
The wet bents bob and sway;
The once warm slippery turf is sodden
Where we laughingly sat or lay.

The summerhouse is gone,
Leaving a weedy space;
The bushes that veiled it once have grown
Gaunt trees that interlace,
Through whose lank limbs I see too clearly
The nakedness of the place.

And where were hills of blue,
Blind drifts of vapour blow,
And the names of former dwellers few,
If any, people know,
And instead of a voice that called, 'Come in, Dears,'
Time calls, 'Pass below!'

394 Life Laughs Onward

RAMBLING I looked for an old abode
Where, years back, one had lived I knew;
Its site a dwelling duly showed,
  But it was new.

I went where, not so long ago,
The sod had riven two breasts asunder;
Daisies throve gaily there, as though
  No grave were under.

I walked along a terrace where
Loud children gambolled in the sun;
The figure that had once sat there
  Was missed by none.

Life laughed and moved on unsubdued,
I saw that Old succumbed to Young:
'Twas well. My too regretful mood
  Died on my tongue.

397 The Wound

I CLIMBED to the crest,
 And, fog-festooned,
The sun lay west
 Like a crimson wound:

Like that wound of mine
 Of which none knew,
For I'd given no sign
 That it pierced me through.

'I WILL get a new string for my fiddle,
  And call to the neighbours to come,
And partners shall dance down the middle
  Until the old pewter-wares hum:
  And we'll sip the mead, cyder, and rum!'

From the night came the oddest of answers:
  A hollow wind, like a bassoon,
And headstones all ranged up as dancers,
  And cypresses droning a croon,
  And gurgoyles that mouthed to the tune.

400 *A January Night*

(1879)

THE rain smites more and more,
The east wind snarls and sneezes;
Through the joints of the quivering door
  The water wheezes.

The tip of each ivy-shoot
Writhes on its neighbour's face;
There is some hid dread afoot
  That we cannot trace.

Is it the spirit astray
Of the man at the house below
Whose coffin they took in to-day?
  We do not know.

402 The Announcement

THEY came, the brothers, and took two chairs
  In their usual quiet way;
And for a time we did not think
  They had much to say.

And they began and talked awhile
  Of ordinary things,
Till spread that silence in the room
  A pent thought brings.

And then they said: 'The end has come.
  Yes: it has come at last.'
And we looked down, and knew that day
  A spirit had passed.

403 The Oxen

CHRISTMAS EVE, and twelve of the clock.
  'Now they are all on their knees,'
An elder said as we sat in a flock
  By the embers in hearthside ease.

We pictured the meek mild creatures where
  They dwelt in their strawy pen,
Nor did it occur to one of us there
  To doubt they were kneeling then.

So fair a fancy few would weave
  In these years! Yet, I feel,
If someone said on Christmas Eve,
  'Come; see the oxen kneel

'In the lonely barton by yonder coomb
  Our childhood used to know,'
I should go with him in the gloom,
  Hoping it might be so.

1915

THE flame crept up the portrait line by line
As it lay on the coals in the silence of night's profound,
  And over the arm's incline,
And along the marge of the silkwork superfine,
And gnawed at the delicate bosom's defenceless round.

Then I vented a cry of hurt, and averted my eyes;
The spectacle was one that I could not bear,
  To my deep and sad surprise;
But, compelled to heed, I again looked furtivewise
Till the flame had eaten her breasts, and mouth, and hair.

'Thank God, she is out of it now!' I said at last,
In a great relief of heart when the thing was done
  That had set my soul aghast,
And nothing was left of the picture unsheathed from the past
But the ashen ghost of the card it had figured on.

She was a woman long hid amid packs of years,
She might have been living or dead; she was lost to my sight,
  And the deed that had nigh drawn tears
Was done in a casual clearance of life's arrears;
But I felt as if I had put her to death that night! . . .

      .   .   .

– Well; she knew nothing thereof did she survive,
And suffered nothing if numbered among the dead;
  Yet – yet – if on earth alive
Did she feel a smart, and with vague strange anguish strive?
If in heaven, did she smile at me sadly and shake her head?

407 An Anniversary

IT was at the very date to which we have come,
   In the month of the matching name,
When, at a like minute, the sun had upswum,
   Its couch-time at night being the same.
And the same path stretched here that people now follow,
   And the same stile crossed their way,
And beyond the same green hillock and hollow
   The same horizon lay;
And the same man pilgrims now hereby who pilgrimed here that
     day.

Let so much be said of the date-day's sameness;
   But the tree that neighbours the track,
And stoops liked a pedlar afflicted with lameness,
   Knew of no sogged wound or wind-crack.
And the joints of that wall were not enshrouded
   With mosses of many tones,
And the garth up afar was not overcrowded
   With a multitude of white stones,
And the man's eyes then were not so sunk that you saw the
     socket-bones.

Kingston-Maurward Ewelease

PORTION of this yew
Is a man my grandsire knew,
Bosomed here at its foot:
This branch may be his wife,
A ruddy human life
Now turned to a green shoot.

These grasses must be made
Of her who often prayed,
Last century, for repose;
And the fair girl long ago
Whom I often tried to know
May be entering this rose.

So, they are not underground,
But as nerves and veins abound
In the growths of upper air,
And they feel the sun and rain,
And the energy again
That made them what they were!

412 *The Last Signal*

(*11 Oct. 1886*)

A Memory of William Barnes

SILENTLY I footed by an uphill road
That led from my abode to a spot yew-boughed;
Yellowly the sun sloped low down to westward,
And dark was the east with cloud.

Then, amid the shadow of that livid sad east,
Where the light was least, and a gate stood wide,
Something flashed the fire of the sun that was facing it,
Like a brief blaze on that side.

Looking hard and harder I knew what it meant –
The sudden shine sent from the livid east scene;
It meant the west mirrored by the coffin of my friend there,
Turning to the road from his green,

To take his last journey forth – he who in his prime
Trudged so many a time from that gate athwart the land!
Thus a farewell to me he signalled on his grave-way,
  As with a wave of his hand.

Winterborne-Came Path

413 *The House of Silence*

'THAT is a quiet place –
That house in the trees with the shady lawn.'
' – If, child, you knew what there goes on
You would not call it a quiet place.
Why, a phantom abides there, the last of its race,
  And a brain spins there till dawn.'

'But I see nobody there, –
Nobody moves about the green,
Or wanders the heavy trees between.'
' – Ah, that's because you do not bear
The visioning powers of souls who dare
  To pierce the material screen.

'Morning, noon, and night,
Mid those funereal shades that seem
The uncanny scenery of a dream,
Figures dance to a mind with sight,
And music and laughter like floods of light
  Make all the precincts gleam.

'It is a poet's bower,
Through which there pass, in fleet arrays,
Long teams of all the years and days,
Of joys and sorrows, of earth and heaven,
That meet mankind in its ages seven,
  An aion in an hour.'

414 Great Things

Sweet cyder is a great thing,
  A great thing to me,
Spinning down to Weymouth town
  By Ridgway thirstily,
And maid and mistress summoning
  Who tend the hostelry:
O cyder is a great thing,
  A great thing to me!

The dance it is a great thing,
  A great thing to me,
With candles lit and partners fit
  For night-long revelry;
And going home when day-dawning
  Peeps pale upon the lea:
O dancing is a great thing,
  A great thing to me!

Love is, yea, a great thing,
  A great thing to me,
When, having drawn across the lawn
  In darkness silently,
A figure flits like one a-wing
  Out from the nearest tree:
O love is, yes, a great thing,
  A great thing to me!

Will these be always great things,
  Great things to me? . . .
Let it befall that One will call,
  'Soul, I have need of thee:'
What then? Joy-jaunts, impassioned flings,
  Love, and its ecstasy,
Will always have been great things,
  Great things to me!

IT pleased her to step in front and sit
   Where the cragged slope was green,
While I stood back that I might pencil it
   With her amid the scene;
      Till it gloomed and rained;
But I kept on, despite the drifting wet
   That fell and stained
My draught, leaving for curious quizzings yet
   The blots engrained.

And thus I drew her there alone,
   Seated amid the gauze
Of moisture, hooded, only her outline shown,
   With rainfall marked across.
      – Soon passed our stay;
Yet her rainy form is the Genius still of the spot,
   Immutable, yea,
Though the place now knows her no more, and has known her not
   Ever since that day.

   From an old note

417 Why Did I Sketch

Why did I sketch an upland green,
    And put the figure in
    Of one on the spot with me? –
For now that one has ceased to be seen
    The picture waxes akin
    To a wordless irony.

If you go drawing on down or cliff
    Let no soft curves intrude
    Of a woman's silhouette,
But show the escarpments stark and stiff
    As in utter solitude;
    So shall you half forget.

Let me sooner pass from sight of the sky
    Than again on a thoughtless day
    Limn, laugh, and sing, and rhyme
With a woman sitting near, whom I
    Paint in for love, and who may
    Be called hence in my time!

From an old note

THE swallows flew in the curves of an eight
     Above the river-gleam
     In the wet June's last beam:
Like little crossbows animate
The swallows flew in the curves of an eight
     Above the river-gleam.

Planing up shavings of crystal spray
     A moor-hen darted out
     From the bank thereabout,
And through the stream-shine ripped his way;
Planing up shavings of crystal spray
     A moor-hen darted out.

Closed were the kingcups; and the mead
     Dripped in monotonous green,
     Though the day's morning sheen
Had shown it golden and honeybee'd;
Closed were the kingcups; and the mead
     Dripped in monotonous green.

And never I turned my head, alack,
     While these things met my gaze
     Through the pane's drop-drenched glaze,
To see the more behind my back. . . .
O never I turned, but let, alack,
     These less things hold my gaze!

LIFELONG to be
Seemed the fair colour of the time;
That there was standing shadowed near
A spirit who sang to the gentle chime
Of the self-struck notes, I did not hear,
  I did not see.

  Thus did it sing
To the mindless lyre that played indoors
As she came to listen for me without:
'O value what the nonce outpours –
This best of life – that shines about
  Your welcoming!'

  I had slowed along
After the torrid hours were done,
Though still the posts and walls and road
Flung back their sense of the hot-faced sun,
And had walked by Stourside Mill, where broad
  Stream-lilies throng.

  And I descried
The dusky house that stood apart,
And her, white-muslined, waiting there
In the porch with high-expectant heart,
While still the thin mechanic air
  Went on inside.

  At whiles would flit
Swart bats, whose wings, be-webbed and tanned,
Whirred like the wheels of ancient clocks:
She laughed a hailing as she scanned
Me in the gloom, the tuneful box
  Intoning it.

  Lifelong to be
I thought it. That there watched hard by
A spirit who sang to the indoor tune,
'O make the most of what is nigh!'
I did not hear in my dull soul-swoon –
  I did not see.

426 On Sturminster Foot-Bridge

(Onomatopœic)

RETICULATIONS creep upon the slack stream's face
 When the wind skims irritably past,
The current clucks smartly into each hollow place
That years of flood have scrabbled in the pier's sodden base;
 The floating-lily leaves rot fast.

On a roof stand the swallows ranged in wistful waiting rows,
 Till they arrow off and drop like stones
Among the eyot-withies at whose foot the river flows:
And beneath the roof is she who in the dark world shows
 As a lattice-gleam when midnight moans.

428 Old Furniture

I KNOW not how it may be with others
 Who sit amid relics of householdry
That date from the days of their mothers' mothers,
  But well I know how it is with me
   Continually.

I see the hands of the generations
 That owned each shiny familiar thing
In play on its knobs and indentations,
  And with its ancient fashioning
   Still dallying:

Hands behind hands, growing paler and paler,
 As in a mirror a candle-flame
Shows images of itself, each frailer
  As it recedes, though the eye may frame
   Its shape the same.

On the clock's dull dial a foggy finger,
 Moving to set the minutes right
With tentative touches that lift and linger
  In the wont of a moth on a summer night,
   Creeps to my sight.

On this old viol, too, fingers are dancing –
    As whilom – just over the strings by the nut,
The tip of a bow receding, advancing
    In airy quivers, as if it would cut
        The plaintive gut.

And I see a face by that box for tinder,
    Glowing forth in fits from the dark,
And fading again, as the linten cinder
    Kindles to red at the flinty spark,
        Or goes out stark.

Well, well. It is best to be up and doing,
    The world has no use for one to-day
Who eyes things thus – no aim pursuing!
    He should not continue in this stay,
        But sink away.

430 *The Last Performance*

'I AM playing my oldest tunes,' declared she,
    'All the old tunes I know, –
Those I learnt ever so long ago.'
– Why she should think just then she'd play them
    Silence cloaks like snow.

When I returned from the town at nightfall
    Notes continued to pour
As when I had left two hours before:
'It's the very last time,' she said in closing;
    'From now I play no more.'

A few morns onward found her fading,
    And, as her life outflew,
I thought of her playing her tunes right through;
And I felt she had known of what was coming,
    And wondered how she knew.

1912

163

'And I saw the figure and visage of Madness seeking for a home'

THERE are three folk driving in a quaint old chaise,
And the cliff-side track looks green and fair;
I view them talking in quiet glee
As they drop down towards the puffins' lair
    By the roughest of ways;
But another with the three rides on, I see,
    Whom I like not to be there!

No: it's not anybody you think of. Next
A dwelling appears by a slow sweet stream
Where two sit happy and half in the dark:
They read, helped out by a frail-wick'd gleam,
    Some rhythmic text;
But one sits with them whom they don't mark,
    One I'm wishing could not be there.

No: not whom you knew and name. And now
I discern gay diners in a mansion-place,
And the guests dropping wit – pert, prim, or choice,
And the hostess's tender and laughing face,
    And the host's bland brow;
But I cannot help hearing a hollow voice,
    And I'd fain not hear it there.

No: it's not from the stranger you met once. Ah,
Yet a goodlier scene than that succeeds;
People on a lawn – quite a crowd of them. Yes,
And they chatter and ramble as fancy leads;
    And they say, 'Hurrah!'
To a blithe speech made; save one, mirthless,
    Who ought not to be there.

Nay: it's not the pale Form your imagings raise,
That waits on us all at a destined time,
It is not the Fourth Figure the Furnace showed;
O that it were such a shape sublime
    In these latter days!
It is that under which best lives corrode;
    Would, would it could not be there!

A Memory of a Sister

THE fire advances along the log
    Of the tree we felled,
Which bloomed and bore striped apples by the peck
    Till its last hour of bearing knelled.

The fork that first my hand would reach
    And then my foot
In climbings upward inch by inch, lies now
    Sawn, sapless, darkening with soot.

Where the bark chars is where, one year,
    It was pruned, and bled –
Then overgrew the wound. But now, at last,
    Its growings all have stagnated.

My fellow-climber rises dim
    From her chilly grave –
Just as she was, her foot near mine on the bending limb,
    Laughing, her young brown hand awave.

December 1915

436 The Caged Goldfinch

WITHIN a churchyard, on a recent grave,
    I saw a little cage
That jailed a goldfinch. All was silence save
    Its hops from stage to stage.

There was inquiry in its wistful eye,
    And once it tried to sing;
Of him or her who placed it there, and why,
    No one knew anything.

439 The Five Students

THE sparrow dips in his wheel-rut bath,
    The sun grows passionate-eyed,
And boils the dew to smoke by the paddock-path;
    As strenuously we stride, –
Five of us; dark He, fair He, dark She, fair She, I,
    All beating by.

The air is shaken, the high-road hot,
    Shadowless swoons the day,
The greens are sobered and cattle at rest; but not
    We on our urgent way, –
Four of us; fair She, dark She, fair He, I, are there,
    But one – elsewhere.

Autumn moulds the hard fruit mellow,
    And forward still we press
Through moors, briar-meshed plantations, clay-pits yellow,
    As in the spring hours – yes,
Three of us; fair He, fair She, I, as heretofore,
    But – fallen one more.

The leaf drops: earthworms draw it in
    At night-time noiselessly,
The fingers of birch and beech are skeleton-thin,
    And yet on the beat are we, –
Two of us; fair She, I. But no more left to go
    The track we know.

Icicles tag the church-aisle leads,
   The flag-rope gibbers hoarse,
The home-bound foot-folk wrap their snow-flaked heads,
   Yet I still stalk the course –
One of us. . . . Dark and fair He, dark and fair She, gone:
   The rest – anon.

441 *During Wind and Rain*

THEY sing their dearest songs –
   He, she, all of them – yea,
Treble and tenor and bass,
      And one to play;
With the candles mooning each face. . . .
      Ah, no; the years O!
How the sick leaves reel down in throngs!

They clear the creeping moss –
   Elders and juniors – aye,
Making the pathways neat
      And the garden gay;
And they build a shady seat. . . .
      Ah, no; the years, the years;
See, the white storm-birds wing across!

They are blithely breakfasting all –
   Men and maidens – yea,
Under the summer tree,
      With a glimpse of the bay,
While pet fowl come to the knee. . . .
      Ah, no; the years O!
And the rotten rose is ript from the wall.

They change to a high new house,
   He, she, all of them – aye,
Clocks and carpets and chairs
      On the lawn all day,
And brightest things that are theirs. . . .
      Ah, no; the years, the years;
Down their carved names the rain-drop ploughs.

THIS after-sunset is a sight for seeing,
Cliff-heads of craggy cloud surrounding it.
  – And dwell you in that glory-show?
You may; for there are strange strange things in being,
    Stranger than I know.

Yet if that chasm of splendour claim your presence
Which glows between the ash cloud and the dun,
  How changed must be your mortal mould!
Changed to a firmament-riding earthless essence
    From what you were of old:

All too unlike the fond and fragile creature
Then known to me. . . . Well, shall I say it plain?
  I would not have you thus and there,
But still would grieve on, missing you, still feature
    You as the one you were.

450 *Who's in the Next Room?*

'WHO's in the next room? – who?
    I seemed to see
Somebody in the dawning passing through,
    Unknown to me.'
'Nay: you saw nought. He passed invisibly.'

'Who's in the next room? – who?
    I seem to hear
Somebody muttering firm in a language new
    That chills the ear.'
'No: you catch not his tongue who has entered there.'

'Who's in the next room? – who?
    I seem to feel
His breath like a clammy draught, as if it drew
    From the Polar Wheel.'
'No: none who breathes at all does the door conceal.'

'Who's in the next room? – who?
          A figure wan
With a message to one in there of something due?
          Shall I know him anon?'
'Yea he; and he brought such; and you'll know him anon.

451 *At a Country Fair*

A T a bygone Western country fair
I saw a giant led by a dwarf
With a red string like a long thin scarf;
How much he was the stronger there
          The giant seemed unaware.

And then I saw that the giant was blind,
And the dwarf a shrewd-eyed little thing;
The giant, mild, timid, obeyed the string
As if he had no independent mind,
          Or will of any kind.

Wherever the dwarf decided to go
At his heels the other trotted meekly,
(Perhaps – I know not – reproaching weakly)
Like one Fate bade that it must be so,
          Whether he wished or no.

Various sights in various climes
I have seen, and more I may see yet,
But that sight never shall I forget,
And have thought it the sorriest of pantomimes,
          If once, a hundred times!

454 Paying Calls

I WENT by footpath and by stile
    Beyond where bustle ends,
Strayed here a mile and there a mile
    And called upon some friends.

On certain ones I had not seen
    For years past did I call,
And then on others who had been
    The oldest friends of all.

It was the time of midsummer
    When they had used to roam;
But now, though tempting was the air,
    I found them all at home.

I spoke to one and other of them
    By mound and stone and tree
Of things we had done ere days were dim,
    But they spoke not to me.

465 Midnight on the Great Western

IN the third-class seat sat the journeying boy,
    And the roof-lamp's oily flame
Played down on his listless form and face,
Bewrapt past knowing to what he was going,
    Or whence he came.

In the band of his hat the journeying boy
    Had a ticket stuck; and a string
Around his neck bore the key of his box,
That twinkled gleams of the lamp's sad beams
    Like a living thing.

What past can be yours, O journeying boy
    Towards a world unknown,
Who calmly, as if incurious quite
On all at stake, can undertake
    This plunge alone?

Knows your soul a sphere, O journeying boy,
    Our rude realms far above,
Whence with spacious vision you mark and mete
This region of sin that you find you in,
        But are not of?

471 *The Clock-Winder*

IT is dark as a cave,
Or a vault in the nave
When the iron door
Is closed, and the floor
Of the church relaid
With trowel and spade.

But the parish-clerk
Cares not for the dark
As he winds in the tower
At a regular hour
The rheumatic clock
Whose dilatory knock
You can hear when praying
At the day's decaying,
Or at any lone while
From a pew in the aisle.

Up, up from the ground
Around and around
In the turret stair
He clambers, to where
The wheelwork is,
With its tick, click, whizz,
Reposefully measuring
Each day to its end
That mortal men spend
In sorrowing and pleasuring.
Nightly thus does he climb
To the trackway of Time.

Him I followed one night
To this place without light,
And, ere I spoke, heard
Him say, word by word,
At the end of his winding,
The darkness unminding: –

'So I wipe out one more,
My Dear, of the sore
Sad days that still be,
Like a drying Dead Sea,
Between you and me!'

Who she was no man knew:
He had long borne him blind
To all womankind;
And was ever one who
Kept his past out of view.

483 *The Shadow on the Stone*

I WENT by the Druid stone
That broods in the garden white and lone,
And I stopped and looked at the shifting shadows
That at some moments fall thereon
From the tree hard by with a rhythmic swing,
And they shaped in my imagining
To the shade that a well-known head and shoulders
Threw there when she was gardening.

I thought her behind my back,
Yea, her I long had learned to lack,
And I said: 'I am sure you are standing behind me,
Though how do you get into this old track?'
And there was no sound but the fall of a leaf
As a sad response; and to keep down grief
I would not turn my head to discover
That there was nothing in my belief.

Yet I wanted to look and see
That nobody stood at the back of me;
But I thought once more: 'Nay, I'll not unvision
A shape which, somehow, there may be.'
So I went on softly from the glade,
And left her behind me throwing her shade,
As she were indeed an apparition –
My head unturned lest my dream should fade.

Begun 1913: finished 1916

487 *The Young Glass-Stainer*

'THESE Gothic windows, how they wear me out
With cusp and foil, and nothing straight or square,
Crude colours, leaden borders roundabout,
And fitting in Peter here, and Matthew there!

'What a vocation! Here do I draw now
The abnormal, loving the Hellenic norm;
Martha I paint, and dream of Hera's brow,
Mary, and think of Aphrodite's form.'

Nov. 1893

493 Men Who March Away

(Song of the Soldiers)

WHAT of the faith and fire within us
    Men who march away
    Ere the barn-cocks say
    Night is growing gray,
Leaving all that here can win us;
What of the faith and fire within us
    Men who march away?

Is it a purblind prank, O think you,
    Friend with the musing eye,
    Who watch us stepping by
    With doubt and dolorous sigh?
Can much pondering so hoodwink you!
Is it a purblind prank, O think you,
    Friend with the musing eye?

Nay. We well see what we are doing,
    Though some may not see –
    Dalliers as they be –
    England's need are we;
Her distress would leave us rueing:
Nay. We well see what we are doing,
    Though some may not see!

In our heart of hearts believing
    Victory crowns the just,
    And that braggarts must
    Surely bite the dust,
Press we to the field ungrieving,
In our heart of hearts believing
    Victory crowns the just.

Hence the faith and fire within us
    Men who march away
    Ere the barn-cocks say
    Night is growing gray,
Leaving all that here can win us;
Hence the faith and fire within us
    Men who march away.

5 September 1914

500 In Time of 'The Breaking of Nations' [1]

I

ONLY a man harrowing clods
    In a slow silent walk
With an old horse that stumbles and nods
    Half asleep as they stalk.

II

Only thin smoke without flame
    From the heaps of couch-grass;
Yet this will go onward the same
    Though Dynasties pass.

III

Yonder a maid and her wight
    Come whispering by:
War's annals will cloud into night
    Ere their story die.

    1915

507 A New Year's Eve in War Time

I

PHANTASMAL fears,
And the flap of the flame,
And the throb of the clock,
And a loosened slate,
And the blind night's drone,
Which tiredly the spectral pines intone!

II

And the blood in my ears
Strumming always the same,
And the gable-cock
With its fitful grate,
And myself, alone.

[1] Jer., LI 20.

III

The twelfth hour nears
Hand-hid, as in shame;
I undo the lock,
And listen, and wait
For the Young Unknown.

IV

In the dark there careers –
As if Death astride came
To numb all with his knock –
A horse at mad rate
Over rut and stone.

V

No figure appears,
No call of my name,
No sound but 'Tic-toc'
Without check. Past the gate
It clatters – is gone.

VI

What rider it bears
There is none to proclaim;
And the Old Year has struck,
And, scarce animate,
The New makes moan.

VII

Maybe that 'More Tears! –
More Famine and Flame –
More Severance and Shock!'
Is the order from Fate
That the Rider speeds on
To pale Europe; and tiredly the pines intone.

1915–1916

I LOOKED up from my writing,
  And gave a start to see,
As if rapt in my inditing,
  The moon's full gaze on me.

Her meditative misty head
  Was spectral in its air,
And I involuntarily said,
  'What are you doing there?'

'Oh, I've been scanning pond and hole
  And waterway hereabout
For the body of one with a sunken soul
  Who has put his life-light out.

'Did you hear his frenzied tattle?
  It was sorrow for his son
Who is slain in brutish battle,
  Though he has injured none.

'And now I am curious to look
  Into the blinkered mind
Of one who wants to write a book
  In a world of such a kind.'

Her temper overwrought me,
  And I edged to shun her view,
For I felt assured she thought me
  One who should drown him too.

HOW it came to an end!
The meeting afar from the crowd,
And the love-looks and laughters unpenned,
The parting when much was avowed,
  How it came to an end!

It came to an end;
Yes, the outgazing over the stream,
With the sun on each serpentine bend,
Or, later, the luring moon-gleam;
  It came to an end.

It came to an end,
The housebuilding, furnishing, planting,
As if there were ages to spend
In welcoming, feasting, and jaunting;
  It came to an end.

It came to an end,
That journey of one day a week:
('It always goes on,' said a friend,
'Just the same in bright weathers or bleak;')
  But it came to an end.

'*How* will come to an end
This orbit so smoothly begun,
Unless some convulsion attend?'
I often said. 'What will be done
  When it comes to an end?'

Well, it came to an end
Quite silently - stopped without jerk;
Better close no prevision could lend;
Working out as One planned it should work
  Ere it came to an end.

When the Present has latched its postern behind my tremulous stay,
  And the May month flaps its glad green leaves like wings,
Delicate-filmed as new-spun silk, will the neighbours say,
  'He was a man who used to notice such things'?

If it be in the dusk when, like an eyelid's soundless blink,
  The dewfall-hawk comes crossing the shades to alight
Upon the wind-warped upland thorn, a gazer may think,
  'To him this must have been a familiar sight.'

If I pass during some nocturnal blackness, mothy and warm,
  When the hedgehog travels furtively over the lawn,
One may say, 'He strove that such innocent creatures should come to
    no harm,
  But he could do little for them; and now he is gone.'

If, when hearing that I have been stilled at last, they stand at the door,
  Watching the full-starred heavens that winter sees,
Will this thought rise on those who will meet my face no more,
  'He was one who had an eye for such mysteries'?

And will any say when my bell of quittance is heard in the gloom,
  And a crossing breeze cuts a pause in its outrollings,
Till they rise again, as they were a new bell's boom,
  'He hears it not now, but used to notice such things'?

523 The Curtains Now Are Drawn

(Song)

I

THE curtains now are drawn,
And the spindrift strikes the glass,
Blown up the jaggèd pass
By the surly salt sou'-west,
And the sneering glare is gone
Behind the yonder crest,
    While she sings to me:
'O the dream that thou art my Love, be it thine,
And the dream that I am thy Love, be it mine,
And death may come, but loving is divine.'

II

I stand here in the rain,
With its smite upon her stone,
And the grasses that have grown
Over women, children, men,
And their texts that 'Life is vain;'
But I hear the notes as when
    Once she sang to me:
'O the dream that thou art my Love, be it thine,
And the dream that I am thy Love, be it mine,
And death may come, but loving is divine.'

1913

I

WHEN moiling seems at cease
    In the vague void of night-time,
    And heaven's wide roomage stormless
    Between the dusk and light-time,
    And fear at last is formless,
We call the allurement Peace.

II

Peace, this hid riot, Change,
    This revel of quick-cued mumming,
    This never truly being,
    This evermore becoming,
    This spinner's wheel onfleeing
Outside perception's range.

  1917

542 *A Night in November*

I MARKED when the weather changed,
And the panes began to quake,
And the winds rose up and ranged,
That night, lying half-awake.

Dead leaves blew into my room,
And alighted upon my bed,
And a tree declared to the gloom
Its sorrow that they were shed.

One leaf of them touched my hand,
And I thought that it was you
There stood as you used to stand,
And saying at last you knew!

  (?) 1913

WHERE three roads joined it was green and fair,
And over a gate was the sun-glazed sea,
And life laughed sweet when I halted there;
Yet there I never again would be.

I am sure those branchways are brooding now,
With a wistful blankness upon their face,
While the few mute passengers notice how
Spectre-bcridden is the place;

Which nightly sighs like a laden soul,
And grieves that a pair, in bliss for a spell
Not far from thence, should have let it roll
Away from them down a plumbless well

While the phasm of him who fared starts up,
And of her who was waiting him sobs from near
As they haunt there and drink the wormwood cup
They filled for themselves when their sky was clear.

Yes, I see those roads – now rutted and bare,
While over the gate is no sun-glazed sea;
And though life laughed when I halted there,
It is where I never again would be.

545 'And There Was a Great Calm'
(On the Signing of the Armistice, 11 Nov. 1918)

I

THERE had been years of Passion – scorching, cold,
And much Despair, and Anger heaving high,
Care whitely watching, Sorrows manifold,
Among the young, among the weak and old,
And the pensive Spirit of Pity whispered, 'Why?'

II

Men had not paused to answer. Foes distraught
Pierced the thinned peoples in a brute-like blindness,
Philosophies that sages long had taught,
And Selflessness, were as an unknown thought,
And 'Hell!' and 'Shell!' were yapped at Lovingkindness.

III

The feeble folk at home had grown full-used
To 'dug-outs', 'snipers', 'Huns', from the war-adept
In the mornings heard, and at evetides perused;
To day-dreamt men in millions, when they mused –
To nightmare-men in millions when they slept.

IV

Waking to wish existence timeless, null,
Sirius they watched above where armies fell;
He seemed to check his flapping when, in the lull
Of night a boom came thencewise, like the dull
Plunge of a stone dropped into some deep well.

V

So, when old hopes that earth was bettering slowly
Were dead and damned, there sounded 'War is done!'
One morrow. Said the bereft, and meek, and lowly,
'Will men some day be given to grace? yea, wholly,
And in good sooth, as our dreams used to run?'

VI

Breathless they paused. Out there men raised their glance
To where had stood those poplars lank and lopped,

As they had raised it through the four years' dance
Of Death in the now familiar flats of France;
And murmured, 'Strange, this! How? All firing stopped?'

VII

Aye; all was hushed. The about-to-fire fired not,
The aimed-at moved away in trance-lipped song.
One checkless regiment slung a clinching shot
And turned. The Spirit of Irony smirked out, 'What?
Spoil peradventures woven of Rage and Wrong?'

VIII

Thenceforth no flying fires inflamed the gray,
No hurtlings shook the dewdrop from the thorn,
No moan perplexed the mute bird on the spray;
Worn horses mused: 'We are not whipped to-day;'
No weft-winged engines blurred the moon's thin horn.

IX

Calm fell. From Heaven distilled a clemency;
There was peace on earth, and silence in the sky;
Some could, some could not, shake off misery:
The Sinister Spirit sneered: 'It had to be!'
And again the Spirit of Pity whispered, 'Why?'

546 Haunting Fingers

A Phantasy in a Museum of Musical Instruments

'ARE you awake,
　　Comrades, this silent night?
　Well 'twere if all of our glossy gluey make
Lay in the damp without, and fell to fragments quite!'

　　'O viol, my friend,
　　　I watch, though Phosphor nears,
　And I fain would drowse away to its utter end
This dumb dark stowage after our loud melodious years!'

And they felt past handlers clutch them,
　　Though none was in the room,
　Old players' dead fingers touch them,
　　　Shrunk in the tomb.

　　' 'Cello, good mate,
　　　You speak my mind as yours:
　Doomed to this voiceless, crippled, corpselike state,
Who, dear to famed Amphion, trapped here, long endures?'

　　'Once I could thrill
　　　The populace through and through,
　Wake them to passioned pulsings past their will.' . . .
(A contra-basso spake so, and the rest sighed anew.)

And they felt old muscles travel
　　Over their tense contours,
　And with long skill unravel
　　　Cunningest scores.

　　'The tender pat
　　　Of her aery finger-tips
　Upon me daily – I rejoiced thereat!'
(Thuswise a harpsichord, as 'twere from dampered lips.)

　　'My keys' white shine,
　　　Now sallow, met a hand
　Even whiter. . . . Tones of hers fell forth with mine
In sowings of sound so sweet no lover could withstand!'

And its clavier was filmed with fingers
  Like tapering flames – wan, cold –
Or the nebulous light that lingers
    In charnel mould.

  'Gayer than most
   Was I,' reverbed a drum;
'The regiments, marchings, throngs, hurrahs! What a host
I stirred – even when crape mufflings gagged me well-nigh dumb!'

    Trilled an aged viol:
   'Much tune have I set free
To spur the dance, since my first timid trial
Where I had birth – far hence, in sun-swept Italy!'

And he feels apt touches on him
  From those that pressed him then;
Who seem with their glance to con him,
    Saying, 'Not again!'

  'A holy calm,'
  Mourned a shawm's voice subdued,
'Steeped my Cecilian rhythms when hymn and psalm
Poured from devout souls met in Sabbath sanctitude.'

  'I faced the sock
  Nightly,' twanged a sick lyre,
'Over ranked lights! O charm of life in mock,
O scenes that fed love, hope, wit, rapture, mirth, desire!'

Thus they, till each past player
  Stroked thinner and more thin,
And the morning sky grew grayer,
    And day crawled in.

HAD I but lived a hundred years ago
I might have gone, as I have gone this year,
By Warmwell Cross on to a Cove I know,
And Time have placed his finger on me there:

'*You see that man?*' – I might have looked, and said,
'O yes: I see him. One that boat has brought
Which dropped down Channel round Saint Alban's Head.
So commonplace a youth calls not my thought.'

'*You see that man?*' – 'Why yes; I told you; yes:
Of an idling town-sort; thin; hair brown in hue;
And as the evening light scants less and less
He looks up at a star, as many do.'

'*You see that man?*' – 'Nay, leave me!' then I plead,
'I have fifteen miles to vamp across the lea,
And it grows dark, and I am weary-kneed:
I have said the third time; yes, that man I see!'

'Good. That man goes to Rome – to death, despair;
And no one notes him now but you and I:
A hundred years, and the world will follow him there,
And bend with reverence where his ashes lie.'

September 1920

NOTE. – In September 1820 Keats, on his way to Rome, landed one
day on the Dorset coast, and composed the sonnet, 'Bright Star!
would I were steadfast as thou art.' The spot of his landing is judged
to have been Lulworth Cove.

'THERE is not much that I can do,
　　For I've no money that's quite my own!'
　　Spoke up the pitying child –
A little boy with a violin
At the station before the train came in, –
'But I can play my fiddle to you,
And a nice one 'tis, and good in tone!'

　　The man in the handcuffs smiled;
The constable looked, and he smiled, too,
　　As the fiddle began to twang;
And the man in the handcuffs suddenly sang
　　　　With grimful glee:
　　　　　'This life so free
　　　　　Is the thing for me!'
And the constable smiled, and said no word,
As if unconscious of what he heard;
And so they went on till the train came in –
The convict, and boy with the violin.

579 *The Rift*

(*Song: Minor Mode*)

'TWAS just at gnat and cobweb-time,
When yellow begins to show in the leaf,
That your old gamut changed its chime
From those true tones – of span so brief! –
That met my beats of joy, of grief,
　　As rhyme meets rhyme.

So sank I from my high sublime!
We faced but chancewise after that,
And never I knew or guessed my crime. . . .
Yes; 'twas the date – or nigh thereat –
Of the yellowing leaf; at moth and gnat
　　And cobweb-time.

THESE flowers are I, poor Fanny Hurd,
            Sir or Madam,
A little girl here sepultured.
Once I flit-fluttered like a bird
Above the grass, as now I wave
In daisy shapes above my grave,
            All day cheerily,
            All night eerily!

– I am one Bachelor Bowring, 'Gent',
            Sir or Madam;
In shingled oak my bones were pent;
Hence more than a hundred years I spent
In my feat of change from a coffin-thrall
To a dancer in green as leaves on a wall,
            All day cheerily,
            All night eerily!

– I, these berries of juice and gloss,
            Sir or Madam,
Am clean forgotten as Thomas Voss;
Thin-urned, I have burrowed away from the moss
That covers my sod, and have entered this yew,
And turned to clusters ruddy of view,
            All day cheerily,
            All night eerily!

– The Lady Gertrude, proud, high-bred,
            Sir or Madam,
Am I – this laurel that shades your head;
Into its veins I have stilly sped,
And made them of me; and my leaves now shine,
As did my satins superfine,
            All day cheerily,
            All night eerily!

– I, who as innocent withwind climb,
            Sir or Madam,
Am one Eve Greensleeves, in olden time
Kissed by men from many a clime,

Beneath sun, stars, in blaze, in breeze,
As now by glowworms and by bees,
   All day cheerily,
   All night eerily![1]

– I'm old Squire Audeley Grey, who grew,
      Sir or Madam,
Aweary of life, and in scorn withdrew;
Till anon I clambered up anew
As ivy-green, when my ache was stayed,
And in that attire I have longtime gayed
   All day cheerily,
   All night eerily!

– And so these maskers breathe to each
      Sir or Madam
Who lingers there, and their lively speech
Affords an interpreter much to teach,
As their murmurous accents seem to come
Thence hitheraround in a radiant hum,
   All day cheerily,
   All night eerily!

[1] It was said her real name was Eve Trevillian or Trevelyan; and that she was the handsome mother of two or three illegitimate children, *circa* 1784–95.

SIR NAMELESS, once of Athelhall, declared:
'These wretched children romping in my park
Trample the herbage till the soil is bared,
And yap and yell from early morn till dark!
Go keep them harnessed to their set routines:
Thank God I've none to hasten my decay;
For green remembrance there are better means
Than offspring, who but wish their sires away.'

Sir Nameless of that mansion said anon:
'To be perpetuate for my mightiness
Sculpture must image me when I am gone.'
– He forthwith summoned carvers there express
To shape a figure stretching seven-odd feet
(For he was tall) in alabaster stone,
With shield, and crest, and casque, and sword complete:
When done a statelier work was never known.

Three hundred years hied; Church-restorers came,
And, no one of his lineage being traced,
They thought an effigy so large in frame
Best fitted for the floor. There it was placed,
Under the seats for schoolchildren. And they
Kicked out his name, and hobnailed off his nose;
And, as they yawn through sermon-time, they say,
'Who was this old stone man beneath our toes?'

YES; such it was;
Just those two seasons unsought,
Sweeping like summertide wind on our ways;
Moving, as straws,
Hearts quick as ours in those days;
Going like wind, too, and rated as nought
Save as the prelude to plays
Soon to come – larger, life-fraught:
Yes; such it was.

'Nought' it was called,
Even by ourselves – that which springs
Out of the years for all flesh, first or last,
Commonplace, scrawled
Dully on days that go past.
Yet, all the while, it upbore us like wings
Even in hours overcast:
Aye, though this best thing of things,
'Nought' it was called!

What seems it now?
Lost: such beginning was all;
Nothing came after: romance straight forsook
Quickly somehow
Life when we sped from our nook,
Primed for new scenes with designs smart and tall. . . .
– A preface without any book,
A trumpet uplipped, but no call;
That seems it now.

614 Lonely Days

LONELY her fate was,
Environed from sight
In the house where the gate was
Past finding at night.
None there to share it,
No one to tell:
Long she'd to bear it,
And bore it well.

Elsewhere just so she
Spent many a day;
Wishing to go she
Continued to stay.
And people without
Basked warm in the air,
But none sought her out,
Or knew she was there.
Even birthdays were passed so,
Sunny and shady:
Years did it last so
For this sad lady.
Never declaring it,
No one to tell,
Still she kept bearing it –
Bore it well.

The days grew chillier,
And then she went
To a city, familiar
In years forespent,
When she walked gaily
Far to and fro,
But now, moving fraily,
Could nowhere go.
The cheerful colour
Of houses she'd known
Had died to a duller
And dingier tone.

Streets were now noisy
Where once had rolled
A few quiet coaches,
Or citizens strolled.
Through the party-wall
Of the memoried spot
They danced at a ball
Who recalled her not.
Tramlines lay crossing
Once gravelled slopes,
Metal rods clanked,
And electric ropes.
So she endured it all,
Thin, thinner wrought,
Until time cured it all,
And she knew nought.

Versified from a Diary

649 *The Whitewashed Wall*

WHY does she turn in that shy soft way
    Whenever she stirs the fire,
And kiss to the chimney-corner wall,
    As if entranced to admire
Its whitewashed bareness more than the sight
    Of a rose in richest green?
I have known her long, but this raptured rite
    I never before have seen.

– Well, once when her son cast his shadow there,
    A friend took a pencil and drew him
Upon that flame-lit wall. And the lines
    Had a lifelike semblance to him.
And there long stayed his familiar look;
    But one day, ere she knew,
The whitener came to cleanse the nook,
    And covered the face from view.

'Yes,' he said: 'My brush goes on with a rush,
    And the draught is buried under;
When you have to whiten old cots and brighten,
    What else can you do, I wonder?'
But she knows he's there. And when she yearns
    For him, deep in the labouring night,
She sees him as close at hand, and turns
    To him under his sheet of white.

663 Waiting Both

A STAR looks down at me,
And says: 'Here I and you
Stand, each in our degree:
What do you mean to do, –
        Mean to do?'

I say: 'For all I know,
Wait, and let Time go by,
Till my change come.' – 'Just so,'
The star says: 'So mean I: –
        So mean I.'

673 Last Week in October

THE trees are undressing, and fling in many places –
On the gray road, the roof, the window-sill –
Their radiant robes and ribbons and yellow laces;
A leaf each second so is flung at will,
Here, there, another and another, still and still.

A spider's web has caught one while downcoming,
That stays there dangling when the rest pass on;
Like a suspended criminal hangs he, mumming
In golden garb, while one yet green, high yon,
Trembles, as fearing such a fate for himself anon.

GONE are the lovers, under the bush
    Stretched at their ease;
    Gone the bees,
Tangling themselves in your hair as they rush
    On the line of your track,
    Leg-laden, back
    With a dip to their hive
    In a prepossessed dive.

Toadsmeat is mangy, frosted, and sere;
    Apples in grass
    Crunch as we pass,
And rot ere the men who make cyder appear.
    Couch-fires abound
    On fallows around,
    And shades far extend
    Like lives soon to end.

Spinning leaves join the remains shrunk and brown
    Of last year's display
    That lie wasting away,
On whose corpses they earlier as scorners gazed down
    From their aery green height:
    Now in the same plight
    They huddle; while yon
    A robin looks on.

ON the frigid face of the heath-hemmed pond
    There shaped the half-grown moon:
Winged whiffs from the north with a husky croon
    Blew over and beyond.

And the wind flapped the moon in its float on the pool,
    And stretched it to oval form;
Then corkscrewed it like a wriggling worm;
    Then wanned it weariful.

And I cared not for conning the sky above
    Where hung the substant thing,
For my thought was earthward sojourning
    On the scene I had vision of.

Since there it was once, in a secret year,
    I had called a woman to me
From across this water, ardently –
    And practised to keep her near;

Till the last weak love-words had been said,
    And ended was her time,
And blurred the bloomage of her prime,
    And white the earlier red.

And the troubled orb in the pond's sad shine
    Was her very wraith, as scanned
When she withdrew thence, mirrored, and
    Her days dropped out of mine.

EVERY branch big with it,
  Bent every twig with it;
Every fork like a white web-foot;
Every street and pavement mute:
Some flakes have lost their way, and grope back upward, whe
Meeting those meandering down they turn and descend again.
  The palings are glued together like a wall,
  And there is no waft of wind with the fleecy fall.

  A sparrow enters the tree,
  Whereon immediately
A snow-lump thrice his own slight size
Descends on him and showers his head and eyes,
  And overturns him,
  And near inurns him,
  And lights on a nether twig, when its brush
Starts off a volley of other lodging lumps with a rush.

  The steps are a blanched slope,
  Up which, with feeble hope,
A black cat comes, wide-eyed and thin;
  And we take him in.

715 Nobody Comes

TREE-LEAVES labour up and down,
    And through them the fainting light
    Succumbs to the crawl of night.
Outside in the road the telegraph wire
    To the town from the darkening land
Intones to travellers like a spectral lyre
    Swept by a spectral hand.

A car comes up, with lamps full-glare,
    That flash upon a tree:
    It has nothing to do with me,
And whangs along in a world of its own,
    Leaving a blacker air;
And mute by the gate I stand again alone,
    And nobody pulls up there.

9 October 1924

735 The Prospect

THE twigs of the birch imprint the December sky
  Like branching veins upon a thin old hand;
I think of summer-time, yes, of last July,
  When she was beneath them, greeting a gathered band
    Of the urban and bland.

Iced airs wheeze through the skeletoned hedge from the north,
  With steady snores, and a numbing that threatens snow,
And skaters pass; and merry boys go forth
  To look for slides. But well, well do I know
    Whither I would go!

December 1912

SHE opened the door of the West to me,
    With its loud sea-lashings,
    And cliff-side clashings
Of waters rife with revelry.

She opened the door of Romance to me,
    The door from a cell
    I had known too well,
Too long, till then, and was fain to flee.

She opened the door of a Love to me,
    That passed the wry
    World-welters by
As far as the arching blue the lea.

She opens the door of the Past to me,
    Its magic lights,
    Its heavenly heights,
When forward little is to see!

1913

753 *Once at Swanage*

THE spray sprang up across the cusps of the moon,
    And all its light loomed green
    As a witch-flame's weirdsome sheen
At the minute of an incantation scene;
And it greened our gaze – that night at demilune.

Roaring high and roaring low was the sea
    Behind the headland shores:
    It symboled the slamming of doors,
Or a regiment hurrying over hollow floors. . . .
And there we two stood, hands clasped; I and she!

786 *The Pat of Butter*

ONCE, at the Agricultural Show,
    We tasted – all so yellow –
    Those butter-pats, cool and mellow!
Each taste I still remember, though
    It was so long ago.

This spoke of the grass of Netherhay,
    And this of Kingcomb Hill,
    And this of Coker Rill:
Which was the prime I could not say
    Of all those tried that day,

Till she, the fair and wicked-eyed,
    Held out a pat to me:
    Then felt I all Yeo-Lea
Was by her sample sheer outvied;
    And, 'This is the best,' I cried.

791 Shortening Days at the Homestead

THE first fire since the summer is lit, and is smoking into the room:
  The sun-rays thread it through, like woof-lines in a loom.
  Sparrows spurt from the hedge, whom misgivings appal
That winter did not leave last year for ever, after all.
    Like shock-headed urchins, spiny-haired,
    Stand pollard willows, their twigs just bared.

Who is this coming with pondering pace,
Black and ruddy, with white embossed,
His eyes being black, and ruddy his face,
And the marge of his hair like morning frost?
      It's the cider-maker,
      And appletree-shaker,
And behind him on wheels, in readiness,
His mill, and tubs, and vat, and press.

796 The Paphian Ball

Another Christmas Experience of the Mellstock Quire

  WE went our Christmas rounds once more,
  With quire and viols as theretofore.

  Our path was near by Rushy-Pond,
  Where Egdon-Heath outstretched beyond.

  There stood a figure against the moon,
  Tall, spare, and humming a weirdsome tune.

  'You tire of Christian carols,' he said:
  'Come and lute at a ball instead.

  ' 'Tis to your gain, for it ensures
  That many guineas will be yours.

  'A slight condition hangs on't, true,
  But you will scarce say nay thereto:

  'That you go blindfold; that anon
  The place may not be gossiped on.'

202

They stood and argued with each other:
'Why sing from one house to another

'These ancient hymns in the freezing night,
And all for nought? 'Tis foolish, quite!'

' – 'Tis serving God, and shunning evil:
Might not elsedoing serve the devil?'

'But grand pay!' . . . They were lured by his call,
Agreeing to go blindfold all.

They walked, he guiding, some new track,
Doubting to find the pathway back.

In a strange hall they found them when
They were unblinded all again.

Gilded alcoves, great chandeliers,
Voluptuous paintings ranged in tiers,

In brief, a mansion large and rare,
With rows of dancers waiting there.

They tuned and played; the couples danced;
Half-naked women tripped, advanced,

With handsome partners footing fast,
Who swore strange oaths, and whirled them past.

And thus and thus the slow hours wore them:
While shone their guineas heaped before them.

Drowsy at length, in lieu of the dance
'*While Shepherds watched . . .*' they bowed by chance;

And in a moment, at a blink,
There flashed a change; ere they could think

The ball-room vanished and all its crew:
Only the well-known heath they view –

The spot of their crossing overnight,
When wheedled by the stranger's sleight.

There, east, the Christmas dawn hung red,
And dark Rainbarrow with its dead

Bulged like a supine negress' breast
Against Clyffe-Clump's faint far-off crest.

Yea; the rare mansion, gorgeous, bright,
The ladies, gallants, gone were quite.

The heaped-up guineas, too, were gone
With the gold table they were on.

'Why did not grasp we what was owed!'
Cried some, as homeward, shamed, they strode.

Now comes the marvel and the warning:
When they had dragged to church next morning,

With downcast heads and scarce a word,
They were astound at what they heard.

Praises from all came forth in showers
For how they'd cheered the midnight hours.

'We've heard you many times,' friends said,
'But like *that* never have you played!

'*Rejoice, ye tenants of the earth,
And celebrate your Saviour's birth,*

'Never so thrilled the darkness through,
Or more inspired us so to do!' . . .

– The man who used to tell this tale
Was the tenor-viol, Michael Mail;

Yes; Mail the tenor, now but earth! –
I give it for what it may be worth.

813 Song to an Old Burden

THE feet have left the wormholed flooring,
    That danced to the ancient air,
    The fiddler, all-ignoring,
Sleeps by the gray-grassed 'cello player:
Shall I then foot around around around,
    As once I footed there!

The voice is heard in the room no longer
    That trilled, none sweetlier,
    To gentle stops or stronger,
Where now the dust-draped cobwebs stir:
Shall I then sing again again again,
    As once I sang with her!

The eyes that beamed out rapid brightness
    Have longtime found their close,
    The cheeks have wanned to whiteness
That used to sort with summer rose:
Shall I then joy anew anew anew,
    As once I joyed in those!

O what's to me this tedious Maying,
    What's to me this June?
    O why should viols be playing
To catch and reel and rigadoon?
Shall I sing, dance around around around,
    When phantoms call the tune!

816 Proud Songsters

THE thrushes sing as the sun is going,
And the finches whistle in ones and pairs,
And as it gets dark loud nightingales
    In bushes
Pipe, as they can when April wears,
    As if all Time were theirs.

These are brand-new birds of twelve-months' growing,
Which a year ago, or less than twain,
No finches were, nor nightingales,
    Nor thrushes,
But only particles of grain,
    And earth, and air, and rain.

818 I Am the One

I AM the one whom ringdoves see
    Through chinks in boughs
    When they do not rouse
    In sudden dread,
But stay on cooing, as if they said:
    'Oh; it's only he.'

I am the passer when up-eared hares,
    Stirred as they eat
    The new-sprung wheat,
    Their munch resume
As if they thought: 'He is one for whom
    Nobody cares.'

Wet-eyed mourners glance at me
    As in train they pass
    Along the grass
    To a hollowed spot,
And think: 'No matter; he quizzes not
    Our misery.'

I hear above: 'We stars must lend
        No fierce regard
        To his gaze, so hard
        Bent on us thus, –
Must scathe him not. He is one with us
        Beginning and end.'

844 *Lying Awake*

YOU, Morningtide Star, now are steady-eyed, over the east,
    I know it as if I saw you;
You, Beeches, engrave on the sky your thin twigs, even the least;
    Had I paper and pencil I'd draw you.

You, Meadow, are white with your counterpane cover of dew,
    I see it as if I were there;
You, Churchyard, are lightening faint from the shade of the yew,
    The names creeping out everywhere.

846 *Childhood among the Ferns*

I SAT one sprinkling day upon the lea,
Where tall-stemmed ferns spread out luxuriantly,
And nothing but those tall ferns sheltered me.

The rain gained strength, and damped each lopping frond,
Ran down their stalks beside me and beyond,
And shaped slow-creeping rivulets as I conned,

With pride, my spray-roofed house. And though anon
Some drops pierced its green rafters, I sat on,
Making pretence I was not rained upon.

The sun then burst, and brought forth a sweet breath
From the limp ferns as they dried underneath:
I said: 'I could live on here thus till death;'

And queried in the green rays as I sate:
'Why should I have to grow to man's estate,
And this afar-noised World perambulate?'

858 The Clasped Skeletons

Surmised Date 1800 B.C.

(In an Ancient British barrow near the writer's house)

O why did we uncover to view
So closely clasped a pair?
Your chalky bedclothes over you,
This long time here!

Ere Paris lay with Helena –
The poets' dearest dear –
Ere David bedded Bathsheba
You two were bedded here.

Aye, even before the beauteous Jael
Bade Sisera doff his gear
And lie in her tent; then drove the nail,
You two lay here.

Wicked Aholah, in her youth,
Colled loves from far and near
Until they slew her without ruth;
But you had long colled here.

Aspasia lay with Pericles,
And Philip's son found cheer
At eves in lying on Thais' knees
While you lay here.

Cleopatra with Antony,
Resigned to dalliance sheer,
Lay, fatuous he, insatiate she,
Long after you'd lain here.

Pilate by Procula his wife
Lay tossing at her tear
Of pleading for an innocent life;
You tossed not here.

Ages before Monk Abélard
Gained tender Héloïse' ear,
And loved and lay with her till scarred,
Had you lain loving here.

So long, beyond chronology,
   Lovers in death as 'twere,
So long in placid dignity
   Have you lain here!

Yet what is length of time? But dream!
   Once breathed this atmosphere
Those fossils near you, met the gleam
   Of day as you did here;

But so far earlier theirs beside
   Your life-span and career,
That they might style of yestertide
   Your coming here!

866 We Field-Women

   How it rained
When we worked at Flintcomb-Ash,
And could not stand upon the hill
Trimming swedes for the slicing-mill.
The wet washed through us – plash, plash, plash:
   How it rained!

   How it snowed
When we crossed from Flintcomb-Ash
To the Great Barn for drawing reed,
Since we could nowise chop a swede. –
Flakes in each doorway and casement-sash:
   How it snowed!

   How it shone
When we went from Flintcomb-Ash
To start at dairywork once more
In the laughing meads, with cows three-score,
And pails, and songs, and love – too rash:
   How it shone!

873 He Never Expected Much

[or]

A Consideration

[A reflection] on My Eighty-Sixth Birthday

WELL, World, you have kept faith with me,
  Kept faith with me;
Upon the whole you have proved to be
  Much as you said you were.
Since as a child I used to lie
Upon the leaze and watch the sky,
Never, I own, expected I
  That life would all be fair.

'Twas then you said, and since have said,
  Times since have said,
In that mysterious voice you shed
  From clouds and hills around:
'Many have loved me desperately,
Many with smooth serenity,
While some have shown contempt of me
  Till they dropped underground.

'I do not promise overmuch,
  Child; overmuch;
Just neutral-tinted haps and such,'
  You said to minds like mine.
Wise warning for your credit's sake!
Which I for one failed not to take,
And hence could stem such strain and ache
  As each year might assign.

874 Standing by the Mantelpiece

(H.M.M., 1873)

THIS candle-wax is shaping to a shroud
To-night. (They call it that, as you may know) –
By touching it the claimant is avowed,
And hence I press it with my finger – so.

To-night. To me twice night, that should have been
The radiance of the midmost tick of noon,
And close around me wintertime is seen
That might have shone the veriest day of June!

But since all's lost, and nothing really lies
Above but shade, and shadier shade below,
Let me make clear, before one of us dies,
My mind to yours, just now embittered so.

Since you agreed, unurged and full-advised,
And let warmth grow without discouragement,
Why do you bear you now as if surprised,
When what has come was clearly consequent?

Since you have spoken, and finality
Closes around, and my last movements loom,
I say no more: the rest must wait till we
Are face to face again, yonside the tomb.

And let the candle-wax thus mould a shape
Whose meaning now, if hid before, you know,
And how by touch one present claims its drape,
And that it's I who press my finger – so.

THREE picture-drawn people stepped out of their frames –
    The blast, how it blew!
And the white-shrouded candles flapped smoke-headed flames;
– Three picture-drawn people came down from their frames,
And dumbly in lippings they told me their names,
    Full well though I knew.

The first was a maiden of mild wistful tone,
    Gone silent for years,
The next a dark woman in former time known;
But the first one, the maiden of mild wistful tone,
So wondering, unpractised, so vague and alone,
    Nigh moved me to tears.

The third was a sad man – a man of much gloom;
    And before me they passed
In the shade of the night, at the back of the room,
The dark and fair woman, the man of much gloom,
Three persons, in far-off years forceful, but whom
    Death now fettered fast.

They set about acting some drama, obscure,
    The women and he,
With puppet-like movements of mute strange allure;
Yea, set about acting some drama, obscure,
Till I saw 'twas their own lifetime's tragic amour,
    Whose course begot me;

Yea – a mystery, ancestral, long hid from my reach
    In the perished years past,
That had mounted to dark doings each against each
In those ancestors' days, and long hid from my reach;
Which their restless enghostings, it seemed, were to teach
    Me in full, at this last.

But fear fell upon me like frost, of some hurt
    If they entered anew
On the orbits they smartly had swept when expert

In the law-lacking passions of life, – of some hurt
To their souls – and thus mine – which I fain would avert;
    So, in sweat cold as dew,

'Why wake up all this?' I cried out. 'Now, so late!
    Let old ghosts be laid!'
And they stiffened, drew back to their frames and numb state,
Gibbering: 'Thus are your own ways to shape, know too late!'
Then I grieved that I'd not had the courage to wait
    And see the play played.

I have grieved ever since: to have balked future pain,
    My blood's tendance foreknown,
Had been triumph. Nights long stretched awake I have lain
Perplexed in endeavours to balk future pain
By uncovering the drift of their drama. In vain,
    Though therein lay my own.

918 *We Are Getting to the End*

WE are getting to the end of visioning
The impossible within this universe,
Such as that better whiles may follow worse,
And that our race may mend by reasoning.

We know that even as larks in cages sing
Unthoughtful of deliverance from the curse
That holds them lifelong in a latticed hearse,
We ply spasmodically our pleasuring.

And that when nations set them to lay waste
Their neighbours' heritage by foot and horse,
And hack their pleasant plains in festering seams,
They may again, – not warely, or from taste,
But tickled mad by some demonic force. –
Yes. We are getting to the end of dreams!

929 The Night of Trafalgar

(*Boatman's Song*)

I

In the wild October night-time, when the wind raved round the land,
And the Back-sea met the Front-sea, and our doors were blocked with
    sand,
And we heard the drub of Dead-man's Bay, where bones of thousands
    are,
We knew not what the day had done for us at Trafalgár.
                    Had done,
                    Had done,
            For us at Trafalgár!

II

'Pull hard, and make the Nothe, or down we go!' one says, says he.
We pulled; and bedtime brought the storm; but snug at home slept we.
Yet all the while our gallants after fighting through the day,
Were beating up and down the dark, sou'-west of Cadiz Bay.
                    The dark,
                    The dark,
            Sou'-west of Cadiz Bay!

III

The victors and the vanquished then the storm it tossed and tore,
As hard they strove, those worn-out men, upon that surly shore;
Dead Nelson and his half-dead crew, his foes from near and far,
Were rolled together on the deep that night at Trafalgár!
                    The deep,
                    The deep,
            That night at Trafalgár!

From 'The Dynasts'

930 Budmouth Dears

(Hussar's Song)

I

WHEN we lay where Budmouth Beach is,
O, the girls were fresh as peaches,
With their tall and tossing figures and their eyes of blue and brown!
And our hearts would ache with longing
As we paced from our sing-songing,
With a smart *Clink! Clink!* up the Esplanade and down.

II

They distracted and delayed us
By the pleasant pranks they played us,
And what marvel, then, if troopers, even of regiments of renown,
On whom flashed those eyes divine, O,
Should forget the countersign, O,
As we tore *Clink! Clink!* back to camp above the town.

III

Do they miss us much, I wonder,
Now that war has swept us sunder,
And we roam from where the faces smile to where the faces frown?
And no more behold the features
Of the fair fantastic creatures,
And no more *Clink! Clink!* past the parlours of the town?

IV

Shall we once again there meet them?
Falter fond attempts to greet them?
Will the gay sling-jacket glow again beside the muslin gown? –
Will they archly quiz and con us
With a sideway glance upon us,
While our spurs *Clink! Clink!* up the Esplanade and down?

From 'The Dynasts'

932 The Eve of Waterloo

(*Chorus of Phantoms*)

THE eyelids of eve fall together at last,
And the forms so foreign to field and tree
Lie down as though native, and slumber fast!

Sore are the thrills of misgiving we see
In the artless champaign at this harlequinade,
Distracting a vigil where calm should be!

The green seems opprest, and the Plain afraid
Of a Something to come, whereof these are the proofs, –
Neither earthquake, nor storm, nor eclipse's shade!

Yea, the coneys are scared by the thud of hoofs,
And their white scuts flash at their vanishing heels,
And swallows abandon the hamlet-roofs.

The mole's tunnelled chambers are crushed by wheels,
The lark's eggs scattered, their owners fled;
And the hedgehog's household the sapper unseals.

The snail draws in at the terrible tread,
But in vain; he is crushed by the felloe-rim;
The worm asks what can be overhead,

And wriggles deep from a scene so grim,
And guesses him safe; for he does not know
What a foul red flood will be soaking him!

Beaten about by the heel and toe
Are butterflies, sick of the day's long rheum,
To die of a worse than the weather-foe.

Trodden and bruised to a miry tomb
Are ears that have greened but will never be gold,
And flowers in the bud that will never bloom.

So the season's intent, ere its fruit unfold,
Is frustrate, and mangled, and made succumb,
Like a youth of promise struck stark and cold! . . .

And what of these who to-night have come?
— The young sleep sound; but the weather awakes
In the veterans, pains from the past that numb;

Old stabs of Ind, old Peninsular aches,
Old Friedland chills, haunt their moist mud bed,
Cramps from Austerlitz; till their slumber breaks.

And each soul shivers as sinks his head
On the loam he's to lease with the other dead
From tomorrow's mist-fall till Time be sped!

From 'The Dynasts'

INDEX OF TITLES

Figures refer to page numbers

INDEX OF FIRST LINES

Figures refer to page numbers

So, Lizbie Browne,
When on a day
Men speak of me
As not, you'll say,
'And who was he?' –
Yes, Lizbie Browne!

99 *A Broken Appointment*

You did not come,
And marching Time drew on, and wore me numb. –
Yet less for loss of your dear presence there
Than that I thus found lacking in your make
That high compassion which can overbear
Reluctance for pure lovingkindness' sake
Grieved I, when, as the hope-hour stroked its sum,
You did not come.

You love not me,
And love alone can lend you loyalty;
– I know and knew it. But, unto the store
Of human deeds divine in all but name,
Was it not worth a little hour or more
To add yet this: Once you, a woman, came
To soothe a time-torn man; even though it be
You love not me?

101 How Great My Grief

(Triolet)

How great my grief, my joys how few,
  Since first it was my fate to know thee
– Have the slow years not brought to view
How great my grief, my joys how few,
Nor memory shaped old times anew,
  Nor loving-kindness helped to show thee
How great my grief, my joys how few,
  Since first it was my fate to know thee?

107 At a Hasty Wedding

(Triolet)

If hours be years the twain are blest,
For now they solace swift desire
By bonds of every bond the best,
If hours be years. The twain are blest
Do eastern stars slope never west,
Nor pallid ashes follow fire:
If hours be years the twain are blest,
For now they solace swift desire.